HEINZ-HARALD
FRENTZEN

Other books by the same author:

JACQUES VILLENEUVE

MICHAEL SCHUMACHER

JOHNNY HERBERT
The Steel behind the Smile

MIKA HAKKINEN
Doing what comes naturally

AYRTON SENNA
His full car racing record

NIGEL MANSELL
The Lion at Bay

GERHARD BERGER
The Human Face of Formula 1

AYRTON SENNA
The Legend Grows

JAMES HUNT
Portrait of a Champion

GRAND PRIX SHOWDOWN!
The full drama of the races which decided the
World Championship 1950–92

TWO WHEEL SHOWDOWN!
The full drama of the races which decided the
World 500cc Motor Cycle Championship from 1949

TORVILL AND DEAN
The full story

JEAN ALESI
Beating the Odds

As part of our ongoing market research, we are always pleased to receive comments about our books, suggestions for new titles, or requests for catalogues. Please write to: The Editorial Director, Haynes Publishing, Sparkford, Nr Yeovil, Somerset BA22 7JJ.

HEINZ-HARALD
FRENTZEN
Back on the pace

CHRISTOPHER HILTON

© Christopher Hilton 1997

First published in 1997

British Library Cataloguing in Publication Data:
A catalogue record for this book is
available from the British Library

ISBN 1 85960 409 9

Library of Congress catalog card no. 97-61068

Haynes Publishing, Sparkford,
Nr Yeovil, Somerset, BA22 7JJ UK.

Tel: 01963 440635 Fax: 01963 440001
Int. tel: +44 1963 440635 Fax: +44 1963 440001

E-mail: sales@haynes-manuals.co.uk
Web site: http://www.haynes.com

Haynes North America, Inc., 861 Lawrence Drive,
Newbury Park, California 91320 USA.

Designed & typeset by G&M, Raunds, Northamptonshire.
Printed and bound in France by Imprimerie Pollina s.a.,
Luçon, France No 73336

Contents

Acknowledgements

THANKS FOR THEIR time and memories to Harald Frentzen (Heinz-Harald's father), Karl Wendlinger, John MacDonald, Jochen Mass, Jochen Neerpasch, Allan McNish, Max Welti and Johnny Herbert of Sauber, Peter Sieber, Albert Hamper, Trevor Foster of Jordan, Allard Kalff and Kees van de Grint.

For finding background and pictures I am indebted to Steve Fellows of *Proaction*, Corinne Wasserfallen of Sauber AG; Lindsay Morle and Jane Gorard of Williams Grand Prix Engineering Limited; Helga Muller, Ford Motor Sport, Cologne; Tanja Severin of Daimler Benz; Regine Michael of Opel; Luki Scheur, Press Officer of the Nurburgring.

Simon Taylor, Chairman of Haymarket Magazines Limited, has kindly given permission for me to use selected extracts from their magazines *Autosport* and *Motoring News*. Both have been invaluable sources. I have quoted from a revealing interview in MAX (MAX Verlag GmbH & Co, Hamburg) and leant heavily on the *Grand Prix Data Book 1997* (Duke) by David Hayhoe and David Holland.

For instant translations I'm indebted to Inga and Barbel. For painstakingly translating much written material – and most of it in motor race-speak – I'm particularly indebted to Birgit Kubisch of Berlin.

Straight
from the grid

A GREY MORNING in an ordinary street on the outskirts of the city: traffic went quietly by, lawnmowers moaned, and the breeze made the leaves whisper politely. The street was called Rheydter Strasse. This was safe suburbia with its pastel-coloured houses strung along both sides, its manicured gardens and its nest of little shops which the distant supermarkets had not yet consumed.

At the far end, in what at first glance appeared to be just such a shop, you see the caskets in the window. They are tastefully arranged, almost as trophies would be, but you cannot mistake what they are for. This is Number 292 and once you've absorbed the caskets you see the name.

FRENTZEN.

The man living in 292, Harald, was very much alive. He chuckled and clucked and laughed and moved constantly as if a great, restless energy was bouncing him around. The young man who used to live in 292, Heinz-Harald, is very much alive and – although calm by nature and difficult to provoke – he was, this summer and autumn of 1997, engaged in a prolonged struggle to prove he was one of the best racing drivers on earth.

Or, as some said, to save his career.

That salvation was formally announced in late September when the Williams team he was driving for confirmed that he would be staying with them in 1998 and added trenchantly: 'With his first season firmly under his belt Heinz-Harald will be in a strong position to challenge for the Championship.' The announcement had been anticipated for a couple of months and so was in the nature of confirmation – but, as we shall see, the 1997 season which

7

promised to be the best of his life proved a merciless examination of the man.

Frank Williams himself expressed delight about the future. 'The new regulations for 1998 will give us a technical challenge and we are confident that the combination of technical expertise and driver continuity will put us in a strong position.'

A world of contrasts. Rheydter Strasse is on the fringe of Moenchengladbach, a solid town on the fringe of the industrial sprawl hewn by coal and steel. The towns have heavy names, Dortmund, Dusseldorf, Duisburg, Essen. Moenchengladbach is also in that area of western Germany which rubs its flank against the Dutch border and is geographically pivotal. Belgium and Luxembourg are just down the road, France nearly within range for nipping down and having lunch.

More or less opposite 292 and high on a wall there was a large hoarding promoting Total petrol. It depicted a young, clean-cut man with a firm jawline who, mute, smiled as he proclaimed the merit of the product. His name was Ralf Schumacher. This was the kid brother of Michael – that Michael who, for nearly a decade, had cast a shadow

The most precious picture. Heinz-Harald Frentzen en route to the first win of his Grand Prix career, at Imola in 1997 (ICN U.K. Bureau).

over Heinz-Harald Frentzen – and, this summer and autumn of 1997, Ralf was in Formula 1 himself.

So now there were three: Heinz-Harald struggling with a Williams, Michael forcing a Ferrari into a strong, sustained bid for his third World Championship, and Ralf doing wild and wonderful things in a Jordan.

The positioning of the hoarding cannot have been deliberate but that didn't alter the fact that, by its very presence, it taunted the Frentzen household. Rhetorically I asked Harald if he had seen it.

'Oh yes!' he said and, far from being offended by the taunting, chuckled and clucked and set off in motion again murmuring 'oh yes!' merry as you like.

A world of contrasts. Only the week before this grey morning Heinz-Harald Frentzen had stalled at the start of the British Grand Prix at Silverstone and then, at the re-start, crashed on the opening lap. Only the week after this grey morning Heinz-Harald would go to the German Grand Prix at Hockenheim and crash on the opening lap. A crisis was upon him, and in a car which ought to have been reaping a great harvest of pole positions, fastest laps and victories – and be well along the way to the World Championship itself by now.

Going in to 1997 he had replaced the current World Champion, Damon Hill, at Williams and the car was expected to be so good – just as it had been for years – that he would surely become World Champion himself (assuming he beat his team-mate Jacques Villeneuve and, naturally, Michael Schumacher). Frentzen knew that many people had made him World Champion before the season even began. He deliberately tried to dampen that but accepted he hadn't managed to. He didn't doubt that he was capable of the championship, but that's quite different from anyone believing it would fall neatly and inevitably into his lap.

Only that week before at Silverstone, Frentzen had sat and explained his situation – or predicament – in controlled terms, pitching the accent towards the positive, which is what Grand Prix drivers are particularly adept at in public. Far from looking worried by what the season was doing to him he said: 'Basically I have reached a level where

Overleaf *Second in France in 1997, a race Michael Schumacher – top right, above Eddie Irvine – won* (ICN U.K. Bureau).

9

I can handle the circumstances around the team to get more out of the car, or the maximum out of the technical ingredients.'

He spoke quietly of the expectations and compared it to a sprinter expected to break the world 100 metre record. Anything less than the record is failure. He had anticipated this, he added, accepted it and was living with it.

Up until then the season had been enough to taunt a man to distraction – not the hoarding opposite Number 292 but real taunting: a brake failure in the season opener at Melbourne when he was running so confidently he might have been announcing – lap after lap, insistent as a hammer – that he was the man to handle this Williams, he was the man to handle this Schumacher; then ninth and a retirement in the two South American rounds, which hinted at – maybe – a crisis developing; then victory at Imola, retirement in Monaco, eighth in Spain, fourth in Canada, second in France so that, reaching Silverstone and the half-way point, it had been a strange season lacking shape, structure or coherence, perhaps.

A world of contrasts. Here he was, now wealthy enough to buy his own plane, struggling to complete a lap rather than a championship. Here he was being told by the magazine MAX 'your media image is that of a bore.' It drew this response: 'Is that what they say, a bore?' (Laughs) 'Actually I don't care about it.'

Why should he care, particularly since he isn't a bore or anything like one. There will be many, many witnesses to that in this book, many testaments to his sense of humour and how he has not permitted what passes for fame and fortune to distort him. Perhaps that's what he meant when he said he didn't care: he is strong enough to know who and what he is, and if other people's perception of him doesn't match that, it's their problem not his.

He has put it with elegant simplicity. 'I am just the way I am and I am not keen on playing a part.'

This is a book about what can go wrong as well as go right. It is a simple tale with complicated side-effects. The simplicity is that, as we shall see, Harald's mother knew how to make fast cars go fast, Harald inherited that from her and Heinz-Harald inherited it from him. What Heinz-Harald really inherited was not just speed but a great natural, instinctive outpouring of it, clean and clear. Others – notably Michael Schumacher – would have to work at it, dissect and analyse it, put all the pieces carefully back together to make their mosaic of how it is reached, how it works when you do reach it.

Frentzen could do it at will.

It became that most curious thing, a precious advantage which simultaneously rubbed along as a disadvantage because doing it at will made the endless dissection and analysis seem unnecessary. We shall see. None of that, however, dilutes the essential premise that the speed (which some found genuinely unbelievable) ought to have reached a natural climax with the Williams drive in Formula 1. The speed had swept him to this summit – but not before tortuous detours, controversy and at least one moment of such bleak despair that he thought of packing the whole thing in and driving a taxi, out of 292.

A world of contrasts. It's time to press the tiny yellow name-button marked FRENTZEN by the door, listen to the bell trilling insistently within, listen to Harald's voice gushing from the intercom next to the button: 'Ah – arrived! Hello! Welcome! Come up!' It's time to step inside so that we can begin at the very beginning, which is – Harald swears – when his first wife Angela was pregnant with Heinz-Harald, she was having driving lessons and Heinz-Harald was *in there* and

Schumacher had always cast a long shadow. This is the Nurburgring in May 1989 before a round of the German Formula 3 Championship (Andreas Stier).

consequently learning to drive at the same time. If such a thing can be true, Heinz-Harald was not born with the skills of speed but rather had already had them for several months when he arrived . . .

This is the sort of notion which enables Harald to fill all the floors of 292 with rippling laughter. However, he was watching me closely as he recounted it to see whether I believed him.

I do, honestly.

In the open plan first floor – lounge/kitchen/dining room – multinational confusion reigns. Harald's third wife is Mexican and it's not absolutely clear to me but apparently she and/or her relatives have arrived at Dusseldorf airport this same grey morning from the overnight Mexico flight. They're all moving and Harald, of course, is moving and everyone is happy. Harald points to the floor which is spread with carpets designed by Heinz-Harald: they are circuit maps and the longer you look at them the better they become, not precisely geometrical but a trifle sensuous.

Then, moving, still moving, Harald gives a conducted tour of the museum he has created to his son's career. It's a low, modern building across the back yard, which is actually a courtyard, and it contains tyres from karting, model cars, posters, a complete corridor of photographic montages – one for each year of the career – pennants, *a Sauber Formula 1 car*, a customised moped, a customised Ford Escort, shelves of cups and everything else Harald has been able to lay hands on.

Harald tries to usher me into a small room crowded with (empty) coffins. He makes a living selling them. 'Yes, yes! Now you see my vehicles without wheels!' He falls into a very serious dissertation on the merits of various makes, explaining his preference for an American version made of metal although he also has the lying-in-state kind with glass apertures.

It was clear then that whatever his son's story would turn out to be, it wouldn't be ordinary.

• CHAPTER ONE •

The bloodline

HARALD FRENTZEN WAS born in what was then the town of Rheydt, now absorbed into the anonymity of Moenchengladbach. He is sure that his own love of speed, which his son inherited, 'comes from my mother and her family, not from my father's side. No, it was my mother's side who were drivers. My father was a student of theology.'

Harald Frentzen finds it interesting how the inheritance from his mother and father has expressed itself among the three children his first wife – Angela, a Spaniard – bore. Heinz-Harald is a racer of course, one daughter teaches English in England, and a second daughter has a diploma in theology.

He summarises the family tree. 'So, from my father's side very studious, from my mother's side drivers! My mother drove, yes. She drove sports cars every time and everywhere she went. She drove only sports cars although she didn't race. It was wartime, you see. After the war she helped me race. She gave me money for my cars, money for my mechanics. My father said *no, I don't like racing*. His life was work, God, praying and then more work. In fact that was his whole life. He knew I was racing because when I finished first he saw it in the newspaper, but he didn't say anything. He was a Christian from a Christian tradition and they do not spend money on racing cars. But my mother liked racing and she paid.'

In the years after the war Harald raced a Porsche and 'we were always first place – gold medal. Only one time we have problems with the engine and were second – silver medal. I raced for pleasure, it was a hobby and I stopped in 1957 because my wife was pregnant with our second child.'

The reason Harald's mother and Harald himself had been able to indulge in expensive cars was morbid in the true sense of the word. The family ran a successful mortuary business. 'My father made coffins, we had a production in coffins,' Harald says.

'There is a story I have to tell, because when Heinz-Harald was in his mother's tummy I told her *if it's a boy I'll give you a car.* She said *but I don't have a licence.* I telephoned a driving instructor and said *please teach my wife to drive, she needs a licence.*' No doubt because she was five months pregnant, a decision was reached that, rather than risk bumping into or being bumped into by other vehicles, she and the instructor would begin the lessons in a saloon car at the karting track of Niederkruchten, which is handily close to Rheydt and near the Dutch border. Technically it's a very difficult track with a lot of corners. 'They went in the afternoon so that she could begin to learn and Heinz-Harald was *in* there!'

Harald also took Angela to the track. 'I made practice with her in a normal car with a gearbox.' It meant that 'every day Heinz-Harald was driving with her but on the inside! She was driving, driving, driving and he was driving!'

Heinz-Harald Frentzen was born on 18 May 1967. 'When he was two or three years old,' Harald says, 'we drove to Spain for a holiday, and he was sitting here on my lap [pretending to drive], not sitting with his mother. He was crazy for the car. We went 2,000 kilometres to Spain and he sat here every day.'

When his son was three Harald provided him with a little go-kart and 'I put him on it.' This was the conversation it provoked:

Heinz-Harald: 'Please can I have a second go-kart.'

'Why?'

Heinz-Harald: 'So I can have races with my friends.'

Harald recalls, 'one week later Heinz-Harald had no tyres left because he was taking corners so quickly.'

Heinz-Harald is happy to admit that he 'always wanted to be a car driver and I couldn't wait until I was old enough. When I was about 10 I had a little kiddie car but I was interested in the technical side of things so I broke up a lawnmower at home and tried to fit the engine to my little car. It didn't work – and nor did the lawnmower after that.'

Harald says 'he came with the lawnmower engine and told me *it's an old one, I need a motor, so please put it in here and I'll be able to go faster.*'

Harald decided, however, that it would 'have been too dangerous to go in the street with, impossible to have done that.'

Thereby hangs another tale, and one surely typical of Harald. It happened when Heinz-Harald was 13. Harald set off to buy a car for his wife. 'I went to the Porsche shop and I saw something there. I said *what's this?* and they said *it's a kart with an engine. We sell them and we have two.*' Harald asked the price and they said *800 marks*.'

Harald could almost hear his son's voice whispering for him to forget the Porsche and get the kart. It worked. 'I came home without the Porsche but with the go-kart. I said *Heinz-Harald, now you have an engine on your kart* and he said *my God!* And that was the beginning. He started at the track at Niederkruchten. After half an hour people watching saw he was so quick they could not believe it and asked how long he had been driving at the track – two years, three?'

Some people, truly, are born to this in the way that others are born pianists or poets; but pianists and poets rarely compete and professionally never in life-threatening situations. Racers do both all the time. Soon enough Heinz-Harald Frentzen was racing karts.

The Frentzen family home in Rheydt. The fan club and their banner obscure the window full of casks (Gunter Passage).

17

'He was born for that,' Harald says. 'He has it in the blood, he can't live without cars, without driving. For example when he began competing we had an American station wagon we'd go to a race in, say, Berlin – 500 kilometres of journey – but he wouldn't sit with the mechanic and me, he sat in the back on the kart, only on the kart, practising.' The mechanic was called Peter Sieber and we'll be meeting him in a moment.

'Frentzen drove a kart like an angel – he didn't need as much practice as anyone else'

In 1981 Frentzen won the West German Junior Cup final. The German magazine *Karting* reported: 'During the timed training Frentzen was ahead by a nose with 54.65 seconds, followed by Thomas Werner with 54.87, Markus Grossmann with 55.10 and Thomas Thunig with 55.17. From pole Frentzen was second at the end of the opening lap behind Werner but in front of Thunig. Next lap Frentzen aquaplaned shortly before he reached the grandstand and his kart spun several times. Thankfully he came to rest parallel to the direction of the race so that the karts arriving from behind were able to shoot past him, albeit at a distance of centimetres.'

Later, 'Werner leads and Grossmann seems to be in a safe second place but Frentzen is approaching, having recovered from a mistake on the first lap. On lap 13 he takes third place from [Joachim] Wessels and attacks Grossmann. On the last lap he has gone past him but then Grossmann is ahead by a nose and finishes second. Despite his misfortune, Frentzen was third.

'During the break for lunch, everybody tried to warm themselves up in the heated restaurant' – this was October – 'and there was no practice for the following open races because the drivers and their helpers were wet enough already.'

Somehow that captures the homely world of karting. Incidentally, Frentzen would meet three of these competitors when he reached German Formula 3 a long way down the road: Frank Schmickler (here sixth), Peter Zakowski (tenth) – Zakowski who late one season would become a potentially devastating spoiler of other people's ambitions, including Frentzen's – and Ellen Lohr (twelfth). A career is like a highway: others are always travelling in the same direction.

Sieber was 'working for Heinz-Harald as his mechanic in 1983 and 1984. We competed in the German and European Championships. I'd been working in karts and one day his father came along and said *you do a good job. Would you like to work for Heinz-Harald?* So OK, I said yes. At the beginning I travelled from my home in Bitburg [about 140 kilometres south] to Moenchengladbach or wherever we were racing but later I lived in the Frentzen house – we shared a big room. I also worked in the family business with Heinz-Harald. I helped everywhere. (I tell Sieber that Harald showed me *the room.* 'Yes, nice!' quoth Sieber, drowning it with enormous laughter.)

'Heinz-Harald was a good person and we had much fun *in the head.* You know what I mean? Jokes! We had a really nice time. In karting he drove a special line, a very clear, clean line. He was excellent. He was quick but you could not see that he was quick, which is always important: the really good ones never look quick, especially when they are quick. It just seems natural. Heinz-Harald drove a kart like an angel. He didn't need as much practice as everyone else. We went to a race at Munich – not a championship although the European champion was competing – and there was no big practice. We did what we could do with our machinery and then he went fastest without the practice and he also won the race. He could just do this.'

Harald remembers this victory in Munich – it was during the Oktoberfest – because it made him 'very, very happy.' Another race produced the same effect. It was at a place no further than 40 kilometres from Moenchengladbach. 'I have a picture from the kart track at Kerpen, 2–3 April 1983. Michael Schumacher was the best at Kerpen, nobody better than him, but Heinz-Harald came to the track and won. Schumacher was second and it was the first time Schumacher had been second.'

Sieber becomes insistent about this race at Kerpen. 'I tell you one thing. In speed Heinz-Harald is maybe quicker than Schumacher, who was completely the opposite: he had to work very hard for his results. He worked very strong with his head in karting and he was excellent technically. Frentzen needed more of a family atmosphere around him. Warmth. That, he needed.'

Here are two themes. The first is the comparison with Schumacher which would pursue Frentzen wherever he went and still pursues him

INFORMATION...No. 14/81

"KCD - CLUB - MEISTERSCHAFT 1981"

ENDSTAND'81 der KCD-JUNIOREN-BUNDES-POKAL MEISTERSCHAFT(JBP):*
(Kl.: J-A/100 mit Z-100-Material,14-16 Jahre ohne Führerschein.)

Bei dieser Aufstellung des Gesamt-End-Ergebnisses'81 sind die zehn
besten und gewerteten Ergebnisse in einer Summe aufgeführt. In
Klammer(-) die Gesamtpunkte-Anzahl der eventl.gestrichenen El-
Ergebnisse. Ausgeschrieben und vorgesehen waren lt.KCD-INFORMA=
TION-Nr.2/81 vom 20.2.81 insgesamt 14 Veranstaltungen(davon 2
Doppelveranstaltungen).Durchgeführt wurden alle 14 End-Läufe(EL).
S i e g e r e h r u n g : 1.-9. Platz im Rahmen der JHV'82 am
27.2.82 in der Stadthalle-Limburg ab 14 Uhr.   (gestr.

		Geb.-Jahrgang+OC.:	...mit +Pt.:	Pt.)
1.	Frentzen,Heinz-H./Mö.Gladbach	*67 OC/16	276	=(21)
2.	Großmann,Markus/Grevenbroich	*66 OC/16	270	=(58)
3.	Werner,Thomas/Althengstedt	*65 OC/35	258	=(30)
4.	Klaffke,Thomas/Nd.-Krüchten	*66 OC/16	243	=(54)
5.	Thunig,Thomas/Kempen	*66 OC/16	238	=(34)
6.	Schmickler,Frank/Köln	*65 OC/11	225	=(54)
7.	Esch,Frank/Wennigsen	*67 KCD-EM	211	=(14)
8.	Walz,Thorsten/Hungen	*67 OC/16	166	=(28)
9.	Goral,Ralf/Duisburg	*67 OC/16	164	=(10)
10.	Zakowski,Peter/Daubach	*66 OC/16	163	=(7)
11.	Wilms,Logan/Wolznach	*67 KCD-EM	156	=(0)
12.	Frl.Lohr,Ellen/Mö.Gladbach	*65 OC/16	155	=(8)
13.	Wilms,Ingo/Wassenberg	*65 OC/16	155	=(8)
14.	Rösser,Udo/Marburg	*66 KCD-EM	147	=(8)
15.	Dauber,Olaf/St.Augusti			
16.	Starck,Guido/Mö.Gladba			
17.	Wessels,Joachim			
18.	Krumbein,Christoph/Gre			
19.	Wagner,Meik/Wittgenbor			
20.	Kassel,Armin/Hagen			
21.	Müller,Hans-J./Stadtal			
22.	Gass,Harald/Schlüchter			
23.	Thielen,Dieter/Kupping			
24.	Velte,Joachim/Pforzhei			
25.	Schröder,Michael/Bedbu			
26.	Suthau,Siegfried/Eschw			
27.	Tassone,Mario/Radolfze			
28.	Weber,Pascal/Dillingen			
29.	Wolf,Michael/Remscheid			
30.	Böhmer,Frank/Wesel			
31.	Otto,Frank/Troisdorf			
32.	Frl.Vorschel,Anke/Kref			
33.	Jäger-Ross,Herbert/Neu			
34.	Held,Klaus/Vöhringen			
35.	Scheydt,Michael/Münche			
36.	Arhelger,Stefan/Haiger			
37.	Wagner,Roland/Nd.-Dorf			
38.	Rust,Frank/Kreuzau			
39.	Zinner,Alexander/Heide			
40.	Dahlmann,Mike/Wetter			

Ffm. d.
7.12.81.
HGSP.:
(R.Böhm)

★ Am "KCD-JBP'82" in der
★ dem Geburtsjahrgang :
★ Im Jahr 1982 scheidet

The Junior Championship result with people Frentzen would meet again later, including Peter Zakowski. Fraulein Ellen Lohr, also from Moenchengladbach, didn't do badly, either.

KARTING

SPORT
INFORMATION
TECHNIK

KART CLUB VON DEUTSCHLAND E.V.
KORPORATIVES MITGLIED DES AvD

| Frankfurt/M. Nr. 11/1981 | Einzelheft DM 3,– | November 1981 | D 21762 E |

Die Goldpokal-Serie
Pokal der Landesmeister
Wetten, daß . . .

Heinz Harald Frentzen, Sieger im KCD-Bundes-Juniorenpokal 1981

Technik und Ausrüstung

German Junior Karting Champion 1981.

IAME
ITAL-AMERICAN MOTOR ENGINEERING

Nr. 1
im Kartsport

EUROKART
A. NEUBERT - 6111 LENGFELD - 06162/2041

today. The second – the need for warmth – will be discussed by current Formula 1 driver Johnny Herbert much later in the book, but is worth bearing in mind meanwhile.

Karting is by no means conclusive evidence of what will happen to a driver's subsequent career in racing cars. For example Frentzen competed in the European Championships at Carpentras, France, in 1984, and the British *Karting* magazine devoted a whole page to the meeting but made only one reference to Frentzen when, in twin vertical columns, they set out the grid for the final. He was on the tenth row and appears simply as 'Frentzen'.

And that's all.

The top five at Carpentras in finishing order were Stefeno Modena, Vincenzo Sospiri, Gert Munkholm, Eric Cheli and Marco Valera. Of these only Modena reached Formula 1. Broadening that, of the 33 starters at this high level of karting only Modena, Frentzen himself and Mika Salo reached Formula 1.

A karting career does not have the closely defined structure of the single-seaters. Kart racing happens all over the place all the time, making it a nightmare for statisticians. The only rational way to try and describe a career is by assembling whatever fragments you can find – generally, by definition, grouped around the major races and championships. Harald sums up: 'We'd spend a week in Australia, a week in South Africa for the Grand Prix there, where he got silver. We have 200 trophies from three years. Karting is every weekend and that's when he raced, every weekend.'

There is a carefully defined time span for a young man remaining in karts, regardless of whether he wins championships or not. After that time he'll remain a karter or find his way to the single-seaters. Frentzen had begun competition karting in 1981 and now it was 1985. He was 18 and he'd covered the span.

During the karting years he'd been noticed by a Dutchman, Kees van de Grint, who worked for the tyre company Bridgestone. Grint

Overleaf – Life at the Summit '97

Main picture *With Williams team-mate Jacques Villeneuve at the Barcelona test in February.*

Top inset *Getting to know the locals in Kyalami, South Africa.*

Bottom inset *The two cars in tandem at Kyalami (all ICN U.K. Bureau).*

remembers many aspects, not least Frentzen having a big crash in South Africa and Harald rushing up and filming him with a video camera rather than dropping the camera and trying to apply first aid! 'This is true.'

Grint's opinion of Frentzen in karting? 'Afterwards it's easy to make judgements but he was the same then as he is now in Formula 1, very quick but never getting the results. That is to say, many times leading but many times retired. People put that down to poor equipment because when the equipment lasted he won, but more often it didn't last.'

'He was the same then as in F1 – very quick but never getting the results'

Is it possible, looking at a youngster karting, to say he will reach Formula 1?

'I don't think so. First of all, karting is a very good training ground but the reason why so many current Formula 1 drivers started there is because they were keen to race and in the early stages of a career the only place you can race is karting! To become a Formula 1 driver you have to have talent and luck. I know two or three karters who were better than anyone else around but they never even made it to Formula 3. The likes of Frentzen, Ayrton Senna, Schumacher, Jos Verstappen and Giancarlo Fisichella were all good but that did not say they would automatically become Formula 1 superstars. Even Senna was not dominant in karts in the way that he was in cars.'

Harald says that he and Heinz-Harald spoke about single-seaters and, once the decision had been taken, Harald decided to form Team Frentzen: 'I was owner, engineer, photographer, publicist and sponsor. Everything.' Well, everything except, as Seiber points, mechanic and truck driver, 'which was me.'

This is how it happened. Seiber recalls: 'The father said *next year we will try Formula Ford 2000* and he bought a car.' Seiber had very little experience of cars – 'a little bit from Hockenheim' – but was asked to stay. 'I explained about my lack of experience and the father said it didn't matter. The father rented a 2000 car from a Mexican, Alfred Toledano, for three or four hours so Heinz-Harald could try it at

Hockenheim.' Toledano had run the car in 1984. Sieber knew Toledano a little bit and the Schubel team, famous in single-seaters, 'taught me a lot, particularly Horst Schubel. So we started in Formula Ford 2000.'

However, while others may have had 1985 cars Frentzen had the 1984.

'The first race was at Zolder,' Sieber says. 'The father told Heinz-Harald OK, *go to the racing drivers' school at Zolder*. It was run by Teddy Pilette [a former Belgian Formula 1 driver]. Zolder is only about three-quarters of an hour from Moenchengladbach. Heinz-Harald arrived in a Porsche, which daddy had organised, and Heinz-Harald said OK, *please teach me how to drive Zolder*. After some laps the teacher looked very bad in the face, Heinz-Harald driving much too quick for him in the Porsche. For the race we had a small tent – like camping – and the car was bigger than the tent! Really it was. The front of the car was out of one side of the tent and the rear out the other.

'Heinz-Harald was always great in the wet, and great in the dry for that matter, but the season was a problem with the material we had [the 1984 car] and money and experience. For example in Zandvoort he was third and then lost that position with a slow puncture. He crashed a lot but I tell you the speed was there. OK, he did have shunts although he learnt quickly. So we had some good results and some bad results, and that first year there were good drivers in Formula Ford 2000, like Bernd Schneider.'

Harald says candidly enough that his son 'did crash many times the first year. Ja, so many times that I said to him *for me you are a Botaniker*,' meaning Heinz-Harald went off the track and ended up examining the greenery, as botanists do.

Frentzen would do a second season in Formula Ford 2000, but this time with the Eifelland team and a man called Albert Hamper. The competition at the top was stiff, with drivers like Ralf Kelleners and Michael Bartels in there.

It is true that Hamper has an enormous sense of humour – he refers to Harald as Old Frentzen and sometimes to Heinz-Harald as Heinz-Harry – and much of what happened still amuses him. For example: 'Old Frentzen is an amazing man. Very nervous. He moves all the time. It was very complicated: in the Formula Ford 2000 time we said to him *don't go over to the car when Heinz-Harald brings it into the pits*' – in other

25

Harald Frentzen shows a promising young driver, Nick Heidfeld, round the museum he has created behind the family home (all Gunter Passage).

words, don't get in the way. 'Every time he went directly to the car. I said *go, please, go to the back of the pits*. The pit door would be closed and he'd come round the front [long laughter].' This does not obscure the fact that Hamper guards a great fondness for Harald Frentzen and some of the stories which follow were related with affection.

'I didn't know them in karting but I heard about it from other guys – like when Heinz-Harald had a big accident in a kart race and Old Frentzen comes with the camera and what did he do? Make photos and Heinz-Harald was not moving and Old Frentzen he do pictures! Very crazy!

'He ran Heinz-Harald in 1986 and it was not so good. In 1986 Old Frentzen did it himself and he made the craziest things on the car. The right [competition] brake pads were too expensive for him so he went to normal stores and bought brake pads. I said to Heinz-Harald *it is a wonder you are still alive!* But Heinz-Harald could drive, and drive anything with four wheels, no problem.

'We had a Reynard car, a brand new car with a new chassis for 1987. Heinz-Harald had no money and Old Frentzen he gave no money! But

Peter Sieber is the man in red (Andreas Stier).

we have the car from Reynard and we spend the winter time all testing on this car and eight days before the first race we stripped it completely, so we didn't test between then and Hockenheim. Heinz-Harald was fifth in qualifying and then in the race had a misfire – a problem with the spark plugs. It was bad and we were fourth.

'The next race was at Zolder, Heinz-Harald qualified second and it was raining. Old Frentzen said *I have good rain tyres, I've had them in my house all winter.*' However, Harald did admit that one tyre of the set wasn't very good and, according to Hamper, had fixed it himself, using a glue called Loctite.

Hamper remembers Harald saying to him 'yes, yes, I made it with Loctite and it's very OK. He can drive with it.' Harald was determined that this was going to happen. Hamper was determined that this was not going to happen.

Hamper said 'he's on pole position and you give him one tyre with Loctite. No! You go to the Bridgestone bus and you buy a new tyre. Minimum one tyre!' Hamper watched from 200 metres away in the paddock as Frentzen went to the bus and came back without a tyre.

'No, not possible, I cannot buy one tyre,' he said.

Hamper said '*I will go with you to Bridgestone* and when we got there I said to them *this man, he wants to buy one tyre for his son.* They said *yes, OK, it's not a problem.* I said *this man, he pays. I buy the tyre but he pays for it . . .*'

Frentzen won the race, his first victory in single-seaters.

Allard Kalff was a young Dutch driver who 'did one race in 1987 in German Formula Ford 2000 – it was at Zolder – when Heinz-Harald was fighting for the Championship and, if I remember right, I finished third. I knew Heinz-Harald because we had a common friend by the name of Henny Vollenberg, who was involved in renting out cars, preparing cars, distributing Bridgestone tyres. He was helping Heinz-Harald at that stage and he was helping me as well, if I got stuck – say, if I needed a set of tyres.

Overleaf – Life at the Summit '97

Main picture *The beginning, Melbourne. Frentzen leads, Villeneuve is in the middle of that sandwich.*

Top inset *Villeneuve and Herbert after the sandwich.*

Bottom inset *Frentzen ought to have had his first win* (all ICN U.K. Bureau).

'I'd met Heinz-Harald during 1986 and 1987 so, at Zolder, it wasn't *who is this guy?* I both knew him and of him. What did I make of him? In those days we all thought *I'm going to Formula 1* and I'm sure he thought the same. It's what you do think as a young driver. Heinz-Harald was prepared to do a lot of work, he'd been preparing his own car and his father was there. His father is a great guy [affectionate chuckling] . . .'

'I told Old Frentzen, if you don't buy rain tyres he stays here until the track is dry'

Nor did Heinz-Harald always spare his father. Hamper remembers, 'one time we were at Zandvoort (fourth round of the 1986 championship) and on the second lap Heinz-Harald made a mistake at the Hugenholtz (the horseshoe left behind the paddock). He went straight into the tyre wall. The car was damaged, he was ashamed, he sat and said nothing. Old Frentzen came up and asked *why* did *you do this and only on the second lap?* Heinz-Harald said *I saw a man in a red jogging outfit and then an arm came from behind me, got hold of the steering wheel and made a right-turn.* And Old Frentzen said *yes, yes,* and then about ten seconds after that he realised and said *expletive Heinz-Harald!!'* The father is a very nice man, he's lovely and crazy.'

The sixth round at Brno, in Czechoslovakia (as it then was) proved to be another saga of wet tyres. 'This was after the damage at Zandvoort,' Hamper says. 'We had to change the car because the 1987 chassis was completely wrecked. Then we go to Czechoslovakia, test and everything was OK. Then in the first timed practice it was raining and we had no rain tyres. I said to Old Frentzen *you buy rain tyres please* but he said *no, too expensive, too expensive.* I said OK, we'll go to the pit lane and wait and see. The weather got better and better and ten minutes before the end of the session all the drivers came in to change from their rain tyres to slicks. Heinz-Harald was in the pits with slicks (of course). Old Frentzen said to him *go on, you must try it* but I said *you don't buy rain tyres, he stays here until the track is dry.*

'Then eight minutes left – a window – and it is dry, well the ideal racing line was dry. I said to Heinz-Harald, OK, *five minutes and out you go, all the others are changing from wets to slicks, you can make a good time.*

He goes out, pulls one and a half seconds over the others, then the session finishes. Old Frentzen says *I told you all the time he didn't need rain tyres!!!* The craziest guy in the whole wide world!'

Kelleners dominated the season with five victories (against Frentzen's two: as well as Zolder he won Mainz). Kelleners finished with 470 points (430 counting), and the scoring system explains how such a massive total could be reached. A win was worth 50 points and points were awarded to the first 25 finishers in a race, which makes you wonder how Paul Jud, a Swiss, managed no more than 16. He was at the bottom of the championship table and the 16 points may be why we have never heard of him since.

Hamper's view of Heinz-Harald as a driver and a young man? 'He was a natural driver. In German we call it natural talent, as you do in English. And as a man he was natural also.'

Capturing what the coming years would bring, Hamper adds: 'Mercedes said to him that he had to do years of testing in saloon cars before he could drive their Group C sports car – *you must do this, do that*. But he said *no, I'm not interested, now I'm going on holiday* [loud laughter from Hamper]. In those days he didn't need to work very hard at the driving. Even when he reached Formula 3 he did nothing, just drove the car, but when he reached Formula 1 with Sauber he started to work hard. Of course he did. I saw him last Sunday [mid-August 1997] at Oschersleben, the new race track in east Germany. I spoke with him and he was exactly as he had been ten years before, always natural, always with jokes.'

Heinz-Harald finished second in the 1987 Formula Ford 2000 Championship and it was time to take the next step. This would be made easier because a very wise and experienced man had been monitoring his progress. He was the last German to have won a Grand Prix, albeit more than a decade before. He was called Jochen Mass.

• CHAPTER TWO •

This easy flair

'WELL, WE DID some driver selection which involved about 30 guys purely to find two for my team. Heinz-Harald was one of the 30. The testing was to enable me to see what the drivers had, and with Heinz-Harald you could tell. It was both the way he drove the car and handled it. What he had was immediately clear: an outstanding talent. So I signed him.'

Jochen Mass, the highly experienced sports car as well as former Formula 1 exponent, was now preparing to run his own team in the new Opel Lotus Challenge – a German Championship of ten rounds with, simultaneously, its equivalent (the GM Vauxhall Lotus) in Britain and, over both of them, an Opel Lotus Euroseries. The idea was to provide authentic racing for youngsters in much the same equipment, which meant that merit rather than technical advantage would be decisive.

Allard Kalff, the young Dutchman we've already met, would compete in the German Championship. He explains that 'the concept of a single make of tyre, a single chassis and a single engine has been widely adopted since. It was good and it still is good. You give everybody the same car and although you'll always have a little bit of difference in engines – a good engine is a good engine, and all the top teams have good engines – it made the racing affordable. That was especially true in the early days, even though it leads to the question, what is affordable in motorsport? Every form is expensive when you go

Right *The Jochen Mass Opel Lotus team – Mass himself and Marco Werner seated next to Frentzen (Opel).*

34

travelling around Europe, and that's what we did. We raced from Portugal to Germany to England – Sweden, even – plus all the domestic German rounds. I think we did 21 races that year but compared to, say, Formula 3, £ for £ it was well spent.'

The cars had Reynard chassis with Opel engines and cost 50,000DM (approximately £20,000). They'd do 0–100kmh in 4.5 seconds and had a top speed of 260kmh. Opel described how 'the single-seaters offer sophisticated machinery and a full opportunity for setting-up and adjusting the cars in the traditional motor racing way. However, strict rules guarantee equality for all competitors. The performance, for instance, of the 155bhp 16-valve engine, which is similar to that of the Opel Kadett GSi 16V, isn't allowed to be changed. Only adjustments of the chassis are allowed.'

Setting up cars is an important, maybe crucial, aspect of preparing for any race. The ability to do it well can be decisive in a successful career, just as an inability can be a constant handicap. It will be a theme of this book.

Kalff says, 'when the first word of Opel Lotus came out in the middle of 1987 Jan Lammers [ex Formula 1 driver] formed a team sponsored by Dutch Opel Dealers and was going to run me and another Dutch guy. Jochen Mass was setting up a team with Heinz-Harald and Marco Werner. There were numerous other teams, but Jochen and Jan, being such experienced racers themselves, were the main ones, they were the people to be with. The first thing which comes to mind about Heinz-Harald in those days was that he was fearless. He probably still is but he had no fear at all then. And he was so quick it was unreal . . .'

Frentzen would be partnered by Werner, from Dortmund, who'd been in Formula Ford 1600 from 1985 to 1987.

The season began in Zolder on 3 April. *Autosport* reported that 'the world debut race of the new Opel Lotus Challenge was won by Dutchman Allard Kalff. Thirty cars took the start and, for 11 of the 15 laps, the race was led by Heinz-Harald Frentzen. He retired with mechanical trouble, handing the win to Kalff.' Frentzen set fastest lap at one minute 40.85 seconds, an average speed of 95.56mph (153kmh).

That same day at Thruxton a young Scot, Allan McNish, won the opening round of the Vauxhall-Lotus Challenge from a young Finn, Mika Hakkinen. 'My first memory of Frentzen,' McNish says, 'was at Thruxton when word came through that he'd led the first German round. In fact I'd never heard of him before.' McNish and Hakkinen would bestride both the British and European rounds but only until Frentzen joined them in the Euroseries.

Frentzen was fourth in Round 2 of the German series at Hockenheim and won Round 3 at the Nurburgring which, one report says, restated the promise he'd demonstrated at the opening round. He led from flag to flag. Kalff, who'd chased hard and drawn up to within 3.35 seconds at the end, was second – enough to protect his Championship lead which stood at 18 points. Werner was third.

'Drivers with so much talent have a handicap – they're always playing'

Frentzen won Round 4 at the Avus circuit in Berlin and was clearly going to be difficult to beat in the Championship, even for Kalff. Opel were putting out press releases laced with excitement. 'Heinz-Harald Frentzen, 21-year-old driver from the Jochen Mass Junior Team, seems to be developing from a champion of qualifying to a serial race winner. After his second victory in a row on the high-speed Avus circuit the fast businessman from Moenchengladbach hopes for a hat-trick in Round 5 on the airport circuit of Mainz-Finthen. On the Avus, the Rhinelander – who started from third position – left his pursuers far behind.

'After this superior victory Frentzen is only two points behind Allard Kalff, who still leads the Championship but had to be satisfied with ninth place on the Avus. Kalff was one of the few drivers who risked rain tyres. Prominent non-finishers included Marco Werner, Jurgen von Gartzen, who was fastest in qualifying, and Hockenheim winner David Luyet from Switzerland. They had been leading the race before they crashed out in an overtaking move on the second lap. They were not hurt.' Opel added that 'pop singer Nino de Angelo finished eighth after having bad luck in the three races before, and he was as happy about this finish as about a Golden Record.'

'The competition was pretty tough,' Mass says, 'and the standard was good,' although Kalff estimates that the competition was 'as it is in any Championship, I suppose. You had four or five quick guys – maybe six – and then quite a few who'd be up there every now and again, and every now and again they wouldn't! A normal Championship, in fact.'

A question to Mass. *What sort of a young man was Frentzen?*

'Well, he had this easy flair of someone with a lot of talent. What made him potentially so outstanding was this: we thought if he could channel his wit into a constructive obsession we'd have a Champion. People who can drive so well so naturally also have a handicap. They don't need to work as hard as the other drivers, they don't have to be as constructive. They are always playing!'

Was that difficult for you?

'No, not really a problem. It might have been right at the beginning but it was quite easy [directing Frentzen] in the sense that his abundance of talent made driving easy for him. Werner was a good driver but a bit too serious, a bit too tense. Werner spoke very openly about the talent of the other guys, Werner is not an envious sort of man but his general outlook on life is pretty dull and that's what didn't help him much. Frentzen, on the other hand, was a happy-go-lucky guy.'

Affordable racing? Before Mainz-Finthen the drivers threatened a boycott over how expensive spare parts were and the consistency of the scrutineering, which perhaps means Opel Lotus was getting properly serious. They raced at Mainz, of course, and Frentzen was second to von Gartzen.

Frentzen won at the Nurburgring, this time from von Gartzen, and contested Round 4 of the Euroseries at Hockenheim, a support race to the German Grand Prix. Opel pointed out that it was the first time drivers in the German Championship had had a chance to take on the Euroseries drivers in front of a home audience. 'The race will take place under strong German participation: 49 drivers have registered, 17 of them German. Challenge-king Frentzen [that's the lovely way they put it] is eagerly awaiting the international fight.' Opel added: 'Also for the first time, pop singer Nino de Angelo will compete against the Euroseries drivers. Perhaps he will have more luck in this than the German Championship, where he has been able to score points only once.'

A question to Kalff. *What was the atmosphere like?*

'Actually, very friendly. For example I remember Allan McNish arriving at Hockenheim for the first time. He'd taken a taxi from Frankfurt Airport to the circuit and was facing a bill of something like

It was a big effort (Opel).

Action at Hockenheim (Opel).

Victory in the GM/Lotus Euroseries in late 1988 at Jerez. Nich Schonstrom (left) was second and Mika Hakkinen (right) third (Opel).

350DM! He came running into the paddock, came over and said *my team's not here. Have you any money so I can pay the taxi driver?* That sort of thing happened. We were all approximately in the same age group, we were all going to places that we'd never been to before and we were all racing. Suddenly there was all this attention and people coming to watch us and it was very good.

'We'd joke around in the paddock and Mika Hakkinen had a mono-bike and we'd play with that. Also EFDA [European Formula Drivers' Association, whose Dan Partel has been in from the beginning] made sure there was no animosity between the teams and any of the drivers. They made sure we all behaved, made sure we were good boys out of the cars, although once we were in the cars it was everybody for himself.'

Frentzen qualified seventh fastest at Hockenheim but had an 'off' in the race.

'There he was, the same man, same sense of humour – he's still a lovely man'

Opel, gazing back at Hockenheim and forward to the next Euroseries round at Spa, said: 'The best results which drivers from the German Championship could achieve in the Euroseries round at Hockenheim were the second and third places of Kalff and von Gartzen. "Actually we can be quite satisfied with this result," said Tony Fall, Sporting Manager of Opel, "in view of the fact that Henrik Larsen dominates the Euroseries and didn't give the other drivers the slightest chance of winning. Our drivers from the German Championship, especially the young Germans themselves, will have to find a way to beat the strong Dane." Especially motivated is Heinz-Harald Frentzen, who was pushed off the track in the very first corner at Hockenheim and therefore had no chance of finishing among the top places. "Henrik Larsen can be beaten and I have proved this with my lap times," says annoyed Frentzen, who made up ground superbly during the race but lost all chance in a second incident.'

Frentzen didn't go to Spa, although Kalff did. 'There were pictures of me in the newspapers flying over the Bus Stop chicane. I tried to make my car into an aeroplane, the way young drivers do. It doesn't work, I can tell you.'

Frentzen was eighth at Zandvoort in the German series. 'The only incident I remember, the only time we physically clashed was at Zandvoort where, if he finished ahead of me, he virtually tied up the Championship,' Kalff says. 'We were running first and second, he began to have a misfire and I was going to overtake him. He thought *well, if you're going to do that you may as well end up in the gravel.* We both went off, but I continued and finished second and he finished low down. It didn't affect our relationship at all. I was a bit angry, as anybody would be, then you think *maybe in his circumstances I'd have acted in the same way, who knows?* So next morning you wake up, it's a new day and off you go again.'

Ordinarily, Kalff points out, 'Heinz-Harald was the hardest one to overtake, full of confidence, hard as a rock but fair, oh yes. In those days I definitely think he was shy but with a lovely sense of humour. He still has that, he hasn't changed. Earlier this year [1997] he was in Holland for a Rothmans promotion. We sat down and had a chat, and there he was, the same man, the same sense of humour. He's still a lovely chap.'

After Zandvoort he won at Spa. This was a German round, which can be a bit confusing. To simplify: the German Championship comprised the ten rounds but four of them were outside Germany (two at Zolder in Belgium, Zandvoort in Holland, Spa in Belgium). This had several advantages, widening the geographical scope and using three circuits which had, or had had, Grand Prix racing. Moreover none was far from Germany.

Now, as Mass says, 'we decided to do some European runs.' That meant contesting the final three rounds of the Euroseries, at the Nurburing, Estoril and Jerez. Of the seven rounds so far, Hakkinen had won four, Larsen two and McNish one.

At the Nurburgring, Frentzen took pole by 0.7 of a second from Werner. In a wet race Frentzen led for three laps before being overtaken by Larsen who established good control by 'coping best with the increasingly damp conditions. Frentzen kept him in sight for the duration, however, and was just behind as they crossed the line after 12 soggy laps. Werner had a lonely run into third' (Opel).

Between that and Estoril, Frentzen faced a German round in Zolder. Opel set the scene. 'If top favourite Frentzen wins, nobody can take the Championship away from him any more, but if von Gartzen – second

Straight line speed in the Opel Lotus series (Motor Sport Aktuel).

The picture McNish remembers so well. The three winners of the respective Opel Lotus championship. (from left) McNish, Frentzen, Hakkinen (Motor Sport Aktuel).

at the moment – or Kalff, third, are successful at Zolder the final decision won't be made until the last round on 16 October at Hockenheim. However, one thing is for sure: the way to the top will lead via Frentzen. From the beginning the 21-year-old has been the strongest driver in this newly-established formula. His qualifying results especially have shown his superiority. Only in Spa did he not start from pole position.'

Before Zolder, Mass confirmed that Frentzen has 'brought experience and fighting spirit into the Lotus cockpit. Already during the tests in the spring I noticed his special talent. It was a very easy decision for me to take him into the team. The same is true of Marco Werner who was less experienced but has become stronger and stronger during the season.'

Frentzen won Zolder.

At Estoril in the Euroseries he took pole again. 'In the second session in less windy conditions Frentzen immediately set the pace, moving into the one minute 39 seconds. No one else came close until the last ten minutes when Hakkinen threw in a one minute 39.911 seconds to challenge Frentzen's 1:39.857. The very next lap Larsen did a one minute 39.910 seconds but then Frentzen put them back in their places with a one minute 39.355 seconds and that was that' (*Autosport*).

Kalff says that Frentzen had 'a couple of very good mechanics around him and he had a very good car, but he made 100% use of it. Some drivers have a very good car and are only able to use it 90%. Take Estoril. None of us had been there before and in qualifying he was so much quicker than everyone else, just like that. It was exactly the sort of thing he could naturally do.'

In the race Frentzen had been 'creeping' while they waited for the green light. 'He was caught out. As he dabbed his brake to curtail the forward motion the light flicked on. Kalff needed no second asking' (*Autosport*). Kalff led for three laps before Frentzen 'dived past under braking into the final hairpin.' Frentzen won it from Larsen by 20 seconds.

Overleaf – Life at the Summit '97

Main picture *The start in Argentina but Frentzen isn't leading – Villeneuve is, and already out of picture.*

Inset *Starting to look serious* (both ICN U.K. Bureau).

At Jerez, a Swede called Niclas Schonstrom took pole, Frentzen 'only' fourth fastest. For the race and 'looking to outfox the opposition, the Mass Team had the tyres on Frentzen's car clad in plastic hoods on the grid. Whether these were for keeping the rubber warm or free from the dust that was blowing everywhere is not known. That they worked is undoubted. The young German made a stormer of a getaway' (*Autosport*) – and won by almost five seconds from Schonstrom.

Astonishingly, he had 56 points from these three Euroseries rounds and that made him sixth in the Championship table.

McNish admits with some candour that 'Frentzen was stunningly quick in the final two rounds and basically walked off into the distance. He beat the regulars hands down. He had a good set-up on the car and he was driving it well. I didn't really speak to him at first. Certainly my German wasn't up to it. His English probably was, but it wasn't that – I don't know what you'd say! I didn't want to be bothered about speaking to him. We did have our pictures taken at Jerez, Mika, myself and Frentzen as the three champions of the whole series, European, British and German. I suppose that was the first time I had a chat with him.'

The final race of the German Championship, at Hockenheim, was also the last of the season. Frentzen said that although he had secured the title he intended to bring his full power to bear here because 'I want to win this one also. It's true it will be what you might call a "free run" for me but as Champion I want to give a fitting final performance.' He gave anything but that.

'Challenge-king Frentzen had some bad luck,' Opel reported diplomatically. 'He was disqualified after he had filled the crowd with enthusiasm, making up ground splendidly and finishing fifth but the fast man from Moenchengladbach had made a little mistake. He had to start the race last because he had been late for the start, failed to notice a red light and was disqualified.'

Autosport of course felt no need for diplomacy. 'Having qualified badly after damaging his car in practice Frentzen had to start from the pit lane. He decided to go before being given the green light and left the pit exit as the middle of the grid went by, causing a hairy moment. The officials took a dim view of this, subsequently removing his fifth place.'

The very next season Frentzen would find himself having to start two races from the pit lane and both times he'd obey the red light. One of those races would cost him a championship.

'Then after 1988,' Mass says, 'we lost him to Formula 3. He had to go there, oh yes, absolutely. He joined Schubel, which was the top team in Germany and still is. Schubel is a good guy, he's got a big company and it was the right move.'

Kees van de Grint worked as what he describes as a 'freelance engineer' with Schubel. 'Everyone knew from Opel Lotus that Heinz-Harald was quite quick – no, extremely quick – but maybe his right foot [on the accelerator] was a little bit faster than his brain in those days! I remember we went testing for the very first time, in Mugello, and within two laps he did a time which he never managed to reach again during the whole week. Unfortunately I must add that on the third lap he crashed the car . . .'

The 1989 German Formula 3 Championship, which would assume hectic and then heroic proportions, essentially involved Frentzen, Schumacher, Michael Bartels and the Austrian Karl Wendlinger. These four grappled with each other for the whole season while, echoing Kalff, other drivers would be up there every now and again.

'Frentzen and Schumacher were side by side in every corner – they eclipsed everyone else'

Wendlinger describes it in similar terms. 'It was a hard fight right from the beginning between Schumacher, Frentzen and me because over the whole season we were the three quickest drivers. Yes, it changed in the sense that there'd be one race where Schumacher was quickest, another where Frentzen was quickest and another where I was. In general, the average performance of the three of us was higher than all the others.'

It began at Hockenheim on 16 April, where Bartels took pole from Schumacher, Frentzen on the sixth row. After the race's 14 laps Frank Kramer won from Ellen Lohr, Schumacher third, Frentzen eleventh. Unusually, it seems, he was not quick instantly – something he began to rectify at the next round, the Nurburgring, where he qualified on the fourth row and finished sixth. There was nearly a genuine sensation. An Argentinian driver called Victor Rosso started on the fourth row of the grid in a Russian-financed car called a Tark Aleko and led for eight laps with Frentzen, Frank Schmickler, Bartels and Schumacher in pursuit and slip-streaming each other furiously. Frentzen's Dallara was

47

evidently not handling well and the slip-streamers slip-streamed by.

At the Avus he qualified on the second row (Schumacher the third, Wendlinger the eighth). From the start six drivers – including Schumacher, Frentzen and Wendlinger – broke away, forming another group of slip-streamers. Wendlinger won, Schumacher third and Frentzen fifth.

At Brno he qualified on the second row although he and Bartels had been highly impressive. The start of the race degenerated into confusion when Frentzen stalled. That meant a re-start which Frentzen had to take from the pit lane. He charged and contemporary reports suggest that his finishing position – ninth – did not reflect either the scope or the scale of the charge.

At Zeltweg Schumacher took pole, Frentzen the third row, but the field spread out around the Osterreichring and Schumacher beat Frentzen by six seconds. The German equivalent to the RAC, the Oberste Nationale Sportkommission, were running a young drivers' scheme and promised the victor of this race a special prize. It guaranteed what Frentzen describes as a 'hard battle.' Grint vividly remembers this as 'an incredible race. It was in the wet and basically Frentzen and Schumacher were side-by-side through every corner. Exciting. Marvellous. They simply eclipsed everybody else.'

At Hockenheim Wendlinger took pole from Schumacher with Frentzen next and an uncompromising race developed. Wendlinger capitalised on the pole position at the green light and led until the second lap when, at the right-hand corner leading into the Stadium section, Frentzen outbraked him – a move which a variety of Formula 1 drivers have tried in Grands Prix over the years with less success than Frentzen, who'd made it safely. Wendlinger ran behind Frentzen and they were joined by a driver called Wolfgang Kaufmann and Schumacher. Then Frentzen opened a gap while Wendlinger and Kaufmann had a proper set-to, banging wheels and taking and re-taking each other until Kaufmann damaged his wing. Schumacher went by, Bartels went by. Frentzen now had a lead of three seconds and although Wendlinger set fastest lap of the race he couldn't catch him.

The Championship was tightening. Schumacher 98 points, Frentzen and Wendlinger 83, Bartels 82, Kaufmann 69. It would inevitably tighten further because of the scoring system. A win was worth 20 points, then, in descending order of places, 18, 16, 15, 14, 13, 12, 11,

The shadow of Schumacher. This is the Nurburgring (Andreas Stier).

The monumental 1989 season in German Formula 3. This is Hockenheim and the finale. (from left) Frentzen, Michael Bartels, You-Know-Who (Andreas Stier).

10, 9, 8, 7, 6, 5, 4, 3, 2, 1. So many points available at each race made it extremely difficult for any driver to build an enormous lead. Schumacher, for example, had needed all his consistency to construct the lead he held: he'd scored in all six rounds and not been lower than fifth. And there might be a twist at the end because only a driver's ten best finishes in the 12 rounds counted.

Qualifying at Wunstorf was lively, Kaufmann pole from Bartels, Wendlinger on the second row, Schumacher on the third, Frentzen on the fourth. The race was lively too. Persistent rain flooded parts of the track. Kaufmann made the strongest start, Bartels and Frentzen after him immediately but Bartels spun off and out. Kaufmann ploughed forward, Frentzen poised, and on lap 5 he outbraked him, then, quite alone, left the rest behind at the rate of some four seconds a lap for a couple of laps. The conditions were now so bad – it was lap 7 – that the race had to be halted, Frentzen leading a driver called Michael Roppes by a huge margin. At the halting: Frentzen 14 minutes 40.16 seconds, Roppes 14 minutes 56.44. Later the race was re-started over a further nine laps, each of which Frentzen led. He beat Wendlinger by more than eight seconds, Schumacher twelfth. The result, on aggregate:

Frentzen	32m 02.13s
Roppes	32m 28.14s
Kaufmann	32m 34.33s
Wendlinger	33m 04.60s

In points, Schumacher 105, Frentzen 103, Wendlinger 98, Kaufmann 85, Bartels 82.

At Hockenheim Frentzen took pole from Wendlinger, Schumacher fourth. Frentzen made a 'blinding' start from Schumacher, who spun at the Ostkurve chicane and later retired with overheating problems. Wendlinger accelerated and, soon enough, was able to exert pressure on Frentzen. These two were travelling so urgently that by lap 2 they'd shed the others and locked into a slip-streaming battle entirely of their own, one darting past on the long straights, the other darting back. The urgency claimed Frentzen who, on lap 4, went off at the Sachskurve, the spoon-shaped corner in the Stadium complex. He took precious seconds to regain the track and when he'd done that Wendlinger had what appeared to be a safe lead. Frentzen went hard after him and it finished tight within the overall tightening:

Easy to forget how good Bartels was, and what might have been (Sports News, Luxembourg).

Action '89, Frentzen off and coming back on (Motor Sport Aktuel).

Wendlinger   31m 17.35s
Frentzen   31m 18.41s with, to show the gap,
Kaufmann   31m 29.17s

The tightening: Frentzen 121, Wendlinger 118, Schumacher 105, Kaufmann 101, Bartels 96.

Grint won't be forgetting this particular race, not least because it was a support to the German Grand Prix and therefore a chance to be noticed. 'Heinz-Harald was twice leading: he spun off, came back on again, led again, spun off again, came back on again but not leading!'

At Diepholz Frentzen took pole from Wendlinger (54.79 seconds against 55.15) with Bartels and Schumacher on the next row (55.26 against 55.28). The race was decided in a flurry of action from the start, Frentzen strongly away, Wendlinger predatory and pressing past. This drew an almost instantaneous response because, at the next corner, Frentzen outbraked Wendlinger and romped off. Schumacher had made anything but a strong start and, after a long and sustained charge, could reach no higher than fourth.

Frentzen   31m 39.70s
Bartels   31m 44.04s
Wendlinger   31m 55.63s
Schumacher   32m 02.45s.

The tightening: Frentzen 141, Wendlinger 134, Schumacher 120, Bartels 114, Kaufmann 101.

Grint won't be forgetting this particular race either. 'At Diepholz, Heinz-Harald dominated but before it we had arguments because I suggested a particular wing setting and he said *no, no. No good at all.* Anyway, we discussed this very strongly and finally he accepted what I was saying and he did dominate – and in great style.'

Now Peter Zakowski was poised to make his move, complicating everything although he only had 81 points. That didn't matter. Zakowski could be that most dangerous and unpredictable of competitors, the spoiler.

The story of the Nurburgring – the first of two consecutive races there but separated by three weeks – can be simply told. Zakowski took pole from Wendlinger, Frentzen on the second row and Schumacher the third. Frentzen started the race from the pit lane and Zakowski won from Wendlinger, Bartels third, Kaufmann fourth, Schumacher fifth, Frentzen seventh. The tightening: Frentzen 153, Wendlinger 152, Schumacher 134, Bartels 130, Kaufmann 116, Zakowski 101.

Telling it simply, however, doesn't do justice to what happened. Grint points out that at this stage the Championship was 'still a battle between Heinz-Harald and Wendlinger. First of all, in practice Heinz-Harald crashed the car. Normal [deep chuckle]. The mechanics had to work all night to repair it. Next morning Heinz-Harald said *good morning* as if nothing had happened. He sat in the car waiting for the warm-up session to begin, everybody went out onto the track but he found it necessary to go to the toilet! He was apparently nervous – though whether he was nervous about damaging the car again I don't know. Anyway, we missed most of the warm-up and he only did a few laps.'

Wanting to do two laps before joining the grid, he sailed down the pit lane, then saw the red light

Then, before the race, Grint was at the grid waiting for Frentzen to arrive at his appointed place on the second row. Frentzen didn't come. 'I called over the radio to the team manager and asked him *have you seen Heinz-Harald?* The team manager said *well as a matter of fact yes, he's just come past along the pit lane!*'

This, Grint thought, was funny-peculiar because, of course, Frentzen should have left the pits long before, completed a leisurely lap and now be settled into that place on the second row. What made it even more funny-peculiar was that if, on the leisurely lap, Frentzen had had a serious problem he'd surely have entered the pit lane but stopped at his pit for emergency repairs. He hadn't. He'd entered the pit lane and sailed past the pit.

The explanation? Grint says that 'because he didn't do all the laps he could have done in the warm-up – which were maybe necessary to get used to the car after the overnight work – he decided to do *two* laps on the way to the grid to get a feel for the car.'

This could be done by going round and – instead of continuing to the grid – entering the pit lane, using that as a conduit, exiting it and going round again, this time culminating in the grid. The team manager had seen Frentzen pass the pit on his way to beginning this second lap. No doubt all would have been well but at a precise time before a race the pit lane is closed: the red light at the end of it comes on and any car still in the pit lane has to stay there and start when the grid has accelerated away.

Frentzen saw . . . the red light.

In the race, Grint says, he was 'catching people, overtaking people,' and seventh place was worth 12 points. This would have a decisive bearing on the whole Championship, and – with only two rounds remaining – we need to examine who'd be dropping what under the eight-best-results-to-count rule.

Frentzen had scored in every round. His lowest points were 8 from Round 1 and 12 from Round 10.

Wendlinger hadn't scored in Round 1, next lowest 15.

Schumacher hadn't scored in Round 8, next lowest 7.

Bartels hadn't scored in Rounds 1 and 7 so that he would keep whatever he got from the last two rounds.

For all practical purposes **Kaufmann** and **Zakowski** were not contenders.

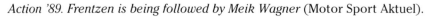

Action '89. Frentzen is being followed by Meik Wagner (Motor Sport Aktuel).

At the second of the consecutive Nurburgring races Schumacher took pole from Wendlinger (1m 15.13s against 1m 15.68s), Bartels and Frentzen on the second row (1m 15.75s against 1m 15.85s). Schumacher led the race throughout while, as *Autosport* reported that Wendlinger, Frentzen and Bartels were 'involved in a first corner crash when Bartels pushed Frentzen from behind. While the latter continued in sixteenth, Bartels had to make a pit-stop to repair a bent wing, while Frentzen and Schmickler had to call it a day.' Frentzen once recounted to me how he'd made a good start, Schumacher ahead, and Bartels 'came into the back of me and pushed me off.'

The tightening: Wendlinger 164, Schumacher 154, Frentzen 153, Kaufmann 134, Bartels 130, Zakowski 117.

It brought these ambitious and fast young men to a shoot-out at Hockenheim on 30 September in Round 12. Only Wendlinger, Schumacher and Frentzen could now become Champion. Amidst the many, many permutations all three had to think in terms of winning the race, and even that might well not be enough for Frentzen. In cold statistics

Wendlinger's 164 would become 172 if he won (dropping 12 from Round 11)

Schumacher's 154 would become 167 if he won (dropping 7 from Round 7)

Frentzen's 153 would become 165 if he won (dropping the 8 from Round 1)

Frentzen took pole by a gasp from Schumacher (1m 01.61s against 1m 01.62), then Zakowski, Bartels, Werner and Wendlinger. Before the race, Frentzen remembers the leading trio were nervous and he estimates Wendlinger more so than he or Schumacher. Wendlinger doesn't agree. In fact, he says, 'I think Frentzen is wrong. I was a bit nervous because we all knew this race was the one which made the decision. I don't think I was more nervous than the other racers. I mean, there is always a little bit of nervousness – but it was not a lot.'

Bartels made the best start with, behind him on the rush to the first corner, Frentzen, Schumacher, Zakowski, Werner, Kaufmann and Wendlinger. In the Stadium section Wendlinger and Kaufmann collided. They pressed on, but at the back. 'I – how can I put it? – lost this race at the beginning but it was not my fault,' says Wendlinger. 'One of our other competitors, who had nothing to do with the

Championship standings, crashed into me and I spun and then I was last. I told myself *you have to race taking the biggest risks and maybe you can save something, because only a top result can help.*'

At the front Bartels and Frentzen were already clear and they drew away from Schumacher. Frentzen tried frantically to get up to Bartels and launch an attack but each time Bartels responded, squeezed, pulled a little way away. Wendlinger charged and had reached ninth when he made a big effort to get past a driver called Frank Kramer. He went off. 'So,' Wendlinger says, 'I took a lot of risks and I got back up the field but there was one guy who didn't let me past. I attacked him a little bit and when I tried to pass him we touched. All this wasn't because I was nervous! Anyway, I bent my suspension and all I could do was cover the last two laps very slowly.'

After the 35 laps it finished

Bartels	36m 55.00s
Frentzen	36m 56.93s
Schumacher	37m 07.41s
Wendlinger (14th)	37m 58.86s

The Championship had finally tightened to this: Wendlinger 164, Frentzen and Schumacher 163, Bartels comparatively distant on 150, Kaufmann lost on 138, Zakowski the spoiler up to 132.

'So Heinz-Harald missed the Championship by one point,' Grint says. 'If he had started from his grid position in that Nurburgring race instead of from the pit lane he would have been Champion. In fact, if he had got one more point he would have been Champion.' That is to say, sixth in the Nurburgring debacle (rather than the seventh) would have given him 13 points against the 12 he did get, so he and Wendlinger would have tied on 164 but Frentzen taken it on the most wins tie-break 3–2.

'Although the Championship was so close,' Grint says, 'the atmosphere was fine. Don't forget that at that time nobody was a star, there were no girlfriend-interferences or anything like that! And if I remember accurately, the atmosphere between the drivers and between the teams was good.'

What sort of a young man was Frentzen?

'Yes [long pause, then a burst of laughter]! At the end of the season I gave him a cartoon I'd had drawn – because he knew best about everything and he had a friend somewhere, a guy called Rudi, and Heinz-Harald would insist to me, for example, *Rudi says this wing is not big enough* or *Rudi says* something else. So I had this cartoon drawn. It was of a car with various things on it but a giant wing.' The caption read

RUDI SAYS . . .

I asked Wendlinger what it was like between him, Schumacher and Frentzen. 'On a personal level it was OK. It was quite a good and normal relationship but not very strong because we didn't know each other very well. There was no contact at all after the races in our private lives. Of course, at the races we saw each other and sometimes we'd have discussions. There were no bad fights, no unfair fights. I

Youthful confidence at the Nurburgring (Andreas Stier).

think that in personal terms and personal behaviour there are differences between all three of us but I don't think it's because they were German and I'm Austrian. You take a couple of Austrian drivers and you still might have differences between all three of us.'

Frentzen contested Macau, where Peter Sieber worked for him. 'He had only one problem at the time: he had the speed but he didn't like to work day and night for racing, he had his other interests. In Macau he was quick but in first practice he had a big shunt so I repaired the monocoque during the night. Nobody regarded Heinz-Harald as a threat. I told him *come on little bastard* [chuckle], *nobody's thinking about you, you have nothing to lose. Now we've got timed practice. You lose all four wheels* [destroy the car] *or we go to the front!* So in the timed practice he went to the front – oversteer, understeer no problem, only on the throttle.' Frentzen qualified fifth, Schumacher incidentally sixth.

'He was leading the race, four seconds in front of Schumacher and he went a little off the racing line – where there was rubber on the track – and had a shunt. Before that, he was so quick. Maybe he lost concentration. I don't know.' In fact he hit the tyre wall on lap 6, marshals were in the process of extracting it when they saw the rest of the field approaching and fled. Frentzen continued and then retired.

As with the dreaded Nurburgring debacle, the story of Macau can be recounted at two levels: the pragmatic (which we've just had, embellished a touch by Sieber) or the panoramic. Let's have that now, from Grint. 'The Schubel team got a big sponsor for Macau. Heinz-Harald's team-mate was Julian Bailey. We went there and everybody was expecting a lot from the team because the sponsor was very big in Macau. I'd been to Macau before with other drivers so I said to Heinz-Harald *shall we take a road car and go through all the corners, have a look at the circuit?* He replied *no, no, no. I've checked the video tape of last year's race.* So I said *well, if you know all the corners, very good.* Anyway, practice starts and there was a very excitable commentator shouting *I see this car going out* and *I see that car going out.* Then he shouted *whooooah. I see a car going off already.* We knew [laughter]. We knew!

'There was a big hole in the carbon monocoque so it was impossible to continue practising. The mechanics were working on the car repairing it. Heinz-Harald said he had had a brake failure. I said to him *you're sure, because it's not very nice to tell the mechanics that.* He said *yeah, yeah. I said OK, we check if it's true and if it's not true we have a problem* – and actually it was not true.'

The explanation wasn't as sinister as that might sound, however.

'Julian Bailey came to me,' Grint continues, 'and asked me *what type of driver is this?* I wondered why. Bailey said *well, in that corner* – I think it was a second gear corner – *there is no way you can take it flat, not even when the car is really well set up, never mind on your first lap.* Heinz-Harald had made a mistake: he got the wrong corner because he thought he was in the next corner, a mild left-hander!'

'I had a good lead and I wanted to see if that corner really was slippery, like you warned'

Hence the imagined brake failure. In fact the brakes hadn't had time to fail because, not knowing the circuit, he'd mistaken this tight corner for the mild version further along . . .

'So he missed the first day of practice and I remember the sponsor's managing director coming down and also asking *what type of a driver is this?* I said with a strong face *well things like this can happen but don't be surprised if he's on pole tomorrow.* This guy said *he'd better be,* and walked away.

'Next day, qualifying started and Heinz-Harald – without any practice and, apart from the video-watching, no knowledge of the circuit – was fifth fastest. So very good. So then I talked to him. I said *listen, this Lisboa corner, which is the one at the end of the straight, you must stay on the inside because the outside is always dirty and slippery – which means you get big understeer and you go off into the tyre wall.* He said OK, *I understand.*'

In summary, the story so far:

'First, damage to the car, then a very good qualifying performance.'

Now, the continuing story:

'The race started, and within a couple of laps he's leading and just pulling away, no problem, then suddenly without any fight he's in the tyre wall. Afterwards – *why?* He said *well, I had a good lead and I wanted to see if the outside of that corner was slippery.* It definitely was, and that was the end of the race.' I asked Grint why a racing driver would want to do that and he professes bemusement. I mention that Schumacher

Moments before the start of the shoot-out at Hockenheim to decide the 1989
Championship – Frentzen, pole, waits for the green light (both Andreas Stier).

wouldn't have risked such an experiment in a thousand years and he
says yes, he's worked with Schumacher, and no, Schumacher wouldn't.
Here, perhaps, is an essential difference distilled.

'I must say in all fairness that the next day or the day after we had a
big party in Hong Kong with the sponsors and he apologised in front of
the mechanics and everybody, so he was fair. At that time he was very,
very quick, most likely the quickest one around but his racing skill was
far behind his pure speed.'

There's an interesting footnote to the 1989 season from Allard Kalff.
After Opel Lotus he went to Britain but it didn't work out so 'I came
back to Holland and Henny Vollenberg said *you should do a race here in
Zandvoort on the Bank Holiday Monday. I've a car, it's Heinz-Harald's
from last year with his settings. All you have to do is get in it and drive it.* I
arrived at the circuit, jumped in the car and finished second or third.
My only thought was *this car is really nice, it's sorted but, wow, it's got too
much understeer in high-speed corners.* At the beginning of 1996 I went to
Japan and drove a Formula 3000 car. The people running it said *well,
the settings on it are the ones Heinz-Harald had when he was racing for us.*

It had quite a bit of understeer as well. It must have been his style of driving – taking a corner really, really quick he'll just drive through the understeer or maybe he doesn't want it to oversteer. I think he's changed that now, but then he was flinging the car into the corners. That's what he got away with in Opel Lotus, that's the way he wanted the car to be and that's how he drove it.'

Some incidentals.

Understeer in a corner can be briefly described as when the rear wheels grip but the front wheels don't. Oversteer is exactly the opposite – and we'll be travelling to Japan soon.

Grint says, 'I liked Heinz-Harald very much, I respected his speed but it could be difficult when we'd meet about settings because basically he wanted to do it his own way. I remember once we were discussing gear ratios and he was telling me how the gearbox worked. I became so upset that I stripped the whole gearbox and told him: *look at it, THAT'S how it works*. Maybe I shouldn't say this but I think in the early years he may have been a little bit spoilt by his father.

'Heinz-Harald is a good human being and I look back on a very memorable time in 1989, a very good time. Of course I was a little bit angry when we lost the Championship but that's all history and I enjoyed the whole year.'

• CHAPTER THREE •

The
wrong turn

THE CREATOR IS called Jochen Neerpasch. 'In 1988, when Mercedes decided to come back to motorsport in a big way, I was part of the strategy group and later on I was responsible for motorsport activities. I was the race director, if you like. We had a medium term strategy to go into a high class of the sport' – the World Sports Car Championship – 'and build up the Sauber organisation and their factory during the sports car races until they could be finally developed into a Formula 1 team. That was the idea from the beginning. At that time Sauber was a small organisation, eight people running a sports car with a Mercedes engine in it.'

A little history to clarify this. Peter Sauber had founded his team in 1970 and it had been a major force in sports car racing for many, many years. Mercedes (and another German team, Auto Union) dominated Grand Prix racing before the Second World War and when Mercedes returned in 1954 they were dominant again. This ended in 1955. Mercedes withdrew from racing in the aftermath of the tragedy at Le Mans that year when one of their cars went into the crowd and 80 people died.

In 1988 Mercedes decided that Sauber, a Swiss team, would literally be the vehicle to take them back into Formula 1 via the sports cars. The long-term strategy was to be in Formula 1 in 1992 or 1993.

Neerpasch says, 'I thought that, to be independent from the market – you never know which good drivers will be available, or which good drivers will be in which teams, or how much they will cost – we should take a decision to develop our own drivers as well as developing Sauber. It was all, let's say, full scale work! We took the best three drivers from the German Formula 3 Championship: Frentzen, Schumacher and Wendlinger. I decided on the three drivers because, first of all, they were different characters. I judged that to be important. Second they were at the top of Formula 3 which, in 1989, was extremely competitive.'

In sum Mercedes would take the trio, known as the Junior Team (or the kids), towards Formula 1 with Sauber via the sports cars. 'Neerpasch is a very nice man and for all three of us he was important at that time,' Wendlinger says. 'He founded the Junior Team and it was a chance for us to . . . well, I don't want to say stop being amateurs, but maybe move from an amateur style of racing to the professional.'

Max Welti was team manager of Sauber. 'The first time I met Heinz-Harald was at a German Formula 3 race in 1989. He could have won that Championship because it was so unbelievably tight between him and Wendlinger, with Michael right in there and Bartels not far away. It was those four guys and they were the ones taken into consideration when we spoke about this Sauber-Mercedes Junior Team. Bartels was considered as well, oh sure. I have to say that the idea of a Junior Team was Neerpasch's. He had already done it once at BMW when he had a junior team of Eddie Cheever, Manfred Winkelhock and Marc Surer so why not try something similar with this obviously talented pair of young Germans and one Austrian?

'It was very, very close between Sauber and Mercedes although it wasn't a Mercedes team, always the Sauber-Mercedes team. The link was so close that we called it the race department of Mercedes – not located in the Mercedes factory at Stuttgart but just outside. Actually Switzerland is only a couple of hours drive from Stuttgart.'

The decision to return to motor racing was announced on 12 January 1988 and that season Sauber ran two cars. One was driven by Jean-Louis Schlesser, Jochen Mass and Mauro Baldi, the other by Baldi and James Weaver. The Junior Team would be brought into being in 1990.

The 1988 cars had the traditional blue Sauber livery and featured their sponsors, AEG, prominently. In 1989 they became silver, the evocative Mercedes racing colours known as The Silver Arrows.

Forming a junior team in sports car racing as a route to Formula 1 was highly unorthodox. The received wisdom insists that to reach Formula 1 you begin in karts and graduate in sequential steps through Formula Ford 1600 or its equivalent, Formula 3 and Formula 3000. The

world of sports cars is quite separate although there is a certain cross-
fertilisation, especially among older drivers. To persuade three young,
aspiring racers to take that route represented a clear risk of their
ambitions being externally misunderstood. Sports cars might be
regarded as an end in itself and, by inference, what the kids wanted
rather than (eventually) Formula 1.

The Junior Team trio would share the driving with Jochen Mass, an
arrangement which allowed them to pursue their single-seater careers
as well. Because there were three of them, it was possible for any two to
be released at any specific time. Hence, for example, Schumacher did a
second season of German Formula 3 and Frentzen did a season of
Formula 3000 with Eddie Jordan Racing. Wendlinger would do a
season of Formula 3000 too.

The risk was minimised because one day Mercedes might well go to
Formula 1, as Sauber or as themselves. I asked Neerpasch if he had told
the kids of the possibility. 'Sure, sure. We did tell this. We didn't tell
them that Mercedes were certain to go into Formula 1 but we did say
there was a good possibility.'

Schumacher once confessed as much when he was vindicating his

Formula 3000 with the Jordan team (Motor Sport Aktuel).

decision to go the sports car route by saying that 'maybe, maybe' Mercedes would re-enter Formula 1 and he'd be on hand if they did.

Mass, who'd monitor, advise and teach the kids, relates with some relish how he was given very little time to make up his mind whether he'd do it or not and was so pleased by the prospect that he only pondered it for about an hour before accepting. He liked the kids, and at his time of life he had nothing much more to prove. 'Don't forget,' he says, 'they were at the beginning and I was at the end so the balance was right.'

Sauber-Mercedes embarked on what Neerpasch describes as 'a very long test period' with the kids in the winter of 1988–89. 'They were the same age, they were very, very competitive against each other and we got them doing more than seven thousand kilometres during the winter. Schlesser and Baldi and Mass were doing the development of the cars with a special engineering team. We always had another car for the Juniors so they could do mileage and go through the different settings. I mean, it was Mercedes, it was a high-class operation and they took what they could get from this.

'They did learn a lot and all three could continue in single-seaters parallel to this continued testing with the sports car, plus doing the sports car races. Mass would always be their partner and the reason for this was that, in single-seaters, each driver is responsible for his own race strategy but, in sports cars, the number one driver has to share the strategy with the number two driver. In that regard they learnt a lot from Mass. They were also learning things like taking different racing lines from single-seaters, learning how to handle the power of the car – it had a lot of power – and much on the engineering side. This was a factory team after all.

'So they were prepared – and being prepared. They went to Willi Dungl [famed fitness guru] in Austria so they were physically and psychologically trained to get the strength which they would need for Formula 1. When they did the testing they didn't care if Schlesser or Baldo or Mass were fast. What was always important to them – what they cared about *underneath* – was how fast the other two Juniors were and how they themselves were developing. That was the real competition.'

Welti says that 'to be honest all I knew about Frentzen was what had been said publicly about him. Human being-wise I had no impression of

Poised even in a static pose: Schumacher and Wendlinger of the Mercedes Junior Team (Mercedes).

Poised, even when listening to Jochen Mass – Schumacher and Wendlinger (Mercedes).

The beautiful Mercedes sports car. Frentzen, Schumacher and Wendlinger were in No. 2 (Mercedes).

him or the others. They were kids: somehow nice, somehow rough, somehow shy, somehow loud, somehow good looking and somehow children. Jochen Mass wasn't given much time to approve it but we knew the kids had to be guided and, from a budget point of view, we could only do it with the three of them.' Bartels was going to be one too many although 'we had had the four of them under consideration.'

I mention to Welti that Mass once told me Frentzen was the 'easiest in'.

'Yes, that's absolutely true.'

Frentzen could just do it, Schumacher was more analytical.

'Look, you have to take this seriously, and do your jokes when you are out of the car'

'I think that's not wrong. What was astonishing was Frentzen's speed from the very beginning. I remember one story of when they were testing for the first time at Paul Ricard [the circuit in the south of France which is a former home of the French Grand Prix] and it happened again at Jerez, where we spent a lot of time: he was sitting in the car and making jokes with the mechanics. He was supposed to be going out to do a quick lap, he had to speed up! I went there as sort of a father figure – because of my age, obviously – and I told him *look, you have to take this seriously and do your jokes when you are out of the car. Concentrate because if you don't, first of all you are not going to be so quick, second of all you're not going to be successful, and third of all you're probably going to destroy the car. That's absolutely what we don't need. We don't have enough material for that blah blah blah.* He said *oh stop that bullshit* or something like that. I was a bit, I won't say angry, but I was a bit upset. He went out and did his first flying lap and it was the quickest . . .'

There are special people who can simply do this, and know they can.

'I think that up to a certain level that's right, but the fact that Michael has been the most successful of the three – without necessarily being the fastest all the time – is not by coincidence. Michael was very quick in the car as well as Frentzen, but in a way he was rough with the material at the beginning. He had huge muscles! He had been wrongly trained – he did a lot of work with weights. He didn't have the smooth driving style that Heinz-Harald had: it was sheer physical strength.

Michael changed that more or less immediately because he is a very, very quick learner, whereas Frentzen has his own attitude, kind of nonchalant and always joking – although he changed very much, too, he turned into a very professional race driver.'

Mass had said there wasn't much to choose between the three of them.

'Michael was more analytical,' Mass explained. 'Michael was trying to work with the car immediately, trying to suss out its weaknesses and strengths, trying to make it more suited to him, so that in the end, of course, he was doing the same speed as Frentzen. And Frentzen, like so many drivers with the talent, hops in, *hoop, a good lap, fine, the car's great*. It can only be a handicap when you have too much talent . . .'

I mentioned to Wendlinger that Mass once told me you took the longest time to get to racing pace.

'In the beginning I was the slowest, yes, for a couple of tests. Then, after that, I was there and I was the one of the Juniors who did the first race, in Suzuka, where my speed was immediately the same as that of Mass. That showed my speed was good. And in testing at the Paul Ricard circuit before that I'd been doing good times. But, yes, in the very beginning – at the first test – I was the slowest because I didn't feel confident in the car: the bad thing you could have done was spin or crash. I was thinking too much about that. Frentzen didn't care at all. He was driving without thinking about any accidents or anything like that.'

This is how the arrangement worked during the 1990 sports car season: **Suzuka** – Mass and Wendlinger, as we've just heard; **Monza** – Mass and Wendlinger; **Silverstone** – Mass and Schumacher; **Spa** – Mass and Wendlinger; **Dijon** – Mass and Schumacher; **Montreal** – Mass and Wendlinger; **Mexico** – Mass and Schumacher. In fact Frentzen's Formula 3000 schedule proved difficult to accommodate. The rounds at Silverstone, Pau, Enna, Brands Hatch, Le Mans and Nogaro clashed, so that he only partnered Mass at **Donington**, 2 September.

There, they qualified on the front row alongside Schlesser and Baldi. *Autosport* reported in summary form: 'First appearance for F3000 man Frentzen. Mass didn't get a good run on Friday, using soft tyres very early. Car improved by end of session. Oil seal blew on Saturday morning, forcing Frentzen to return to pits with minor engine bay fire.

Left *Frentzen* did *drive this Mercedes* (Gunter Passage).

Car out of action for rest of day, so Mass used spare to improve time. Electronic problems with refettled race car in warm-up, so forced to use spare car for race.'

Mass took the first stint but the car slewed at the opening corner – Redgate – and went sideways on the final corner, making him third. Baldi moved away at the rate of a second a lap, Mass trapped behind Julian Bailey (Nissan). Mass needed until lap 8 to overtake Bailey so that, at 10 laps, Baldi led Mass by 8 seconds. Mass stabilised it there and then handed the car to Frentzen who locked into a battle with Martin Brundle (Jaguar).

On lap 53, *Autosport* reported that Frentzen was 'on the Jag's tail. Coming out of the Esses Frentzen blasted by into second place but hesitated on the way into Melbourne Hairpin allowing Brundle to sneak back inside. On the pit straight Frentzen tried again and pulled alongside – incredibly the Olivetti/Longines timing beam recorded the gap at 0.000 seconds! Frentzen, on the left, cheekily tried to chop across and forced Brundle onto the grass. When Brundle held his ground and came steaming down to Redgate on the inside line Frentzen thought better of it, and let the Jag back through. Next time round he tried again at Melbourne and made it safely. This caused Brundle to comment that he would send Mercedes a bill for training the young drivers . . .'

Welti, reflecting, says that 'it is fair to say the Junior Team was a great success. You look at the results – and all three subsequently reached Formula 1. The kids were doing their share, yes they were, absolutely.'

Do you feel that Frentzen progressed during the year?

'Unfortunately Heinz-Harald did not progress during that year. He progressed during that winter period when we were doing something like the 7,000 kilometres and the three were always together.'

Frentzen did tell me it was difficult for them because, courtesy of the telemetry, they couldn't conceal anything from each other.

Overleaf – Life at the Summit '97

Main picture *Victory at San Marino: the start.*

Inset *Decorum on the podium, the shadow of Schumacher still there* (both ICN U.K. Bureau).

'For the first time in their lives they were driving with telemetry and that was very new to them. There was no cheating.'

Was there a deliberate attempt to create stress between them?

'No. I think it was not necessary. That was taken into consideration, but actually it really did end up not being necessary. They wanted to have success so much that it took care of itself.'

Frentzen said that, of the three of them, Wendlinger was somehow an outsider.

'Karl was the outsider because he was basically calmer than the other two and he was the slowest learner. Karl is a different character. It took him the longest amount of time until he was quick, whereas Heinz-Harald was quick immediately – whether he'd slept or he hadn't slept, whether he was in a good mood or a bad mood. He just got in the car and *bang*. Michael had to learn it. I mean, Michael had less experience in motor racing than Frentzen, who'd won the Opel Lotus Championship already. Frentzen's speed was, and I believe still is, unbelievable.'

I mentioned about the telemetry to Wendlinger, he partially misunderstood but his answer is extremely interesting. 'I see it a bit differently because at that time we were very young boys in a professional team. We were driving but we weren't setting up the car, we weren't playing with the telemetry like we did afterwards in Formula 1 and now even in saloon cars.'

No, what Frentzen told me was that you could look at the telemetry and see who was fast where, and who wasn't.

'Yes, we could but if I remember right, at the beginning it was just driving. The plan from Jochen Neerpasch and Peter Sauber was to take away as much pressure as possible and one thing was not to show us the telemetry because if one of the guys was quickest in Signes [the right-hander at the end of the long straight at Ricard] then the other two go crazy to go quicker! That created a greater risk that somebody would crash the car and the most important thing was to avoid that. It is correct what Neerpasch told you, that we would put pressure on ourselves. There was no pressure at all from the team.'

Meanwhile Sauber were growing according to the strategy, their workforce increasing from 8 to 75. Clearly Formula 1 was becoming more and more of a probability.

Meanwhile Frentzen did the 1990 season with Jordan too, and how

74

he arrived there is a story within itself. Trevor Foster, Jordan race director, says 'we didn't really know him. We'd seen a little bit of him in the German Formula 3 Championship and kept abreast of what he was doing. He was brought to us by Henny Vollenburg, who had been his manager-type person if you like, and he'd also support from Camel Germany as an individual market – as opposed to the Camel global group who we were sponsored by. They pushed Eddie very hard to run a three-car 3000 team, which is what we did.' Eddie Irvine and Emanuele Naspetti were the others.

'He was fast, but he couldn't give the engineers any direction – feedback was minimal'

'The thing about Heinz-Harald is that he is a really, really nice chap. A super guy. Very, very friendly, very down to earth. I think that all he knew was that he could drive a racing car but he didn't always know where the time [meaning speed which gained him time] came from, so therefore when the time wasn't there he didn't know where it had gone either. He'd get in the car, go out and literally within eight or nine laps that was as fast as that car was going to go. Unless you, as an engineer, found something to make it happen, something to make him or allow him to go faster, that was it: that was the limit.

'If you did find something he would exploit it, oh yes, absolutely, but you had to find it. He couldn't give you a direction. It was very, very minimal feedback. He was competitive: he wanted to be as fast as Irvine, who'd already done a year of 3000. Naspetti was also in his second year and was quite strong at certain races but never hit a level of consistency.

'Frentzen could not understand why he wasn't as quick as Irvine therefore it was *oh, my engine's no good, it must be my engine that's down on power* or it was *maybe my monocoque's no good, maybe it's a flexing monocoque* and all that.

'For example we went to Hockenheim [the seventh round] and it totally blew him away. He could not understand why Irvine was dicing for pole position and eventually qualified third while he was down in fifteenth place, nowhere near on Irvine's pace. Even Irvine would say *Heinz-Harald is braking so late going into the chicanes, he's sorting the car*

75

Left *The young man armed with Camel money* (Gunter Passage).

out in the middle of the chicanes, he's late on the power and can't get out of the chicanes. [Hockenheim is a high-speed autobahn containing three chicanes and how you handle them is vital.] Eddie said *I'm braking earlier than he is and I'm cleaner through the chicanes.*

'We talked to Heinz-Harald quite a bit at Hockenheim to try and get him to change his driving style, but he couldn't. There was one way he knew: you braked as late as you physically could, you got the car through the corner somehow, and you kept the thing going. He was strong on the street circuits – Birmingham and Pau – where you drive on total reflexes because the corners are blind and you are using all your car control, all your natural ability.

'Sadly I don't think he had the capacity to take him to the next level. It was the concentration factor out of the car. You couldn't hold the concentration for very long on any point of issue, like how can we go faster tomorrow? He'd say, *well, you know, the brakes are fading.* You'd say *we've got the biggest brake ducts on, we've got the hardest brake pads* but he'd repeat *well the brakes are fading.* That was it. There was nothing more he could say – like *I'll brake ten yards earlier and find a way of regaining the speed.* No. That was it.

'The problem is that you've got to stay there when you've finished a day's testing or whatever. You've got to stay there until you are happy that you have found the answers to enable you to go quicker tomorrow. It's no good getting out of the car, saying to the engineers *well it's six o'clock and I'm going, find me half a second for tomorrow.*

'At Hockenheim I remember his engineer coming to me and saying Heinz-Harald was complaining of oversteer everywhere. The engineer said *I have tried this, I have tried that, tried the other thing, nothing makes any difference.* I said *right, we will give him a set-up which should almost make the car oversteer off the circuit.* It should literally have ploughed straight on – a most dramatic sort of change to make. Next morning I asked his engineer what did Heinz-Harald reckon to that? He related how Heinz-Harald said *still the same.* It didn't matter what you did with it. If he needed to turn the car a bit harder he would just turn it harder, almost regardless of set-up. This was a classic case where, to help him, we changed the car more out of frustration than anything else and he came into the pits and was it better? *Still the same.* He couldn't feel it, couldn't feel if it was any better.

'It was Hockenheim when he was complaining about the engine. We then took him to Birmingham and the street race and – with the same engine, same chassis, same car – he outqualified Irvine. That proved that he just got in the car and drove it.

'The problem with testing was that you couldn't go testing! We didn't have the data analysis then that we have now [and were thus more reliant on what the driver said]. The car had a set-up on it, he went out, there was a lap time – *I might be able to find a tenth of a second* – but you couldn't say *well, let's try these front dampers* or *these rear dampers,* or *let's try these roll bars . . .*'

Was that frustrating?

'Very much so because he was naturally very fast and if you happened to get the car with the right set-up on the day he would do a damn good job for you. But it needed more than that, and if we are comparing him to Michael Schumacher he is nowhere near as complete.'

It must also be said that Frentzen, who finished joint sixteenth on three points, crashed a time or two. He spun off at Donington, had an accident at Pau, crashed at Monza, had an accident in Birmingham, had an accident at Le Mans, whilst at Nogaro he didn't qualify for the race.

I mention to Foster about the crashing.

'Yes. He was over-driving – because of the frustrations, because he couldn't understand why he wasn't quicker, because he couldn't understand why his team-mates were. He'd think *the only thing I can do is try harder.* Obviously there is a limit for everything. You go over it – well some drivers are going to get away with it more than others, but in the end you're always going to get caught out, aren't you? He'd over-drive because he was following the only way he knew of how to make the car go faster.'

McNish was racing for the DAMS team that season. 'Summing up,' he says, 'Heinz-Harald was very, very quick but ragged. He was quickest on some occasions, although that wasn't taken for read. It was certainly recognised that the likelihood of him finishing a race was not that high. Irvine was in the same team and Irvine, while not as blindingly quick over one lap, knew the circuits and knew what was coming up and was more consistent. Heinz-Harald wasn't able to harness the speed he generated and he threw good situations away. I think in 1990 he lost confidence. It didn't bother me because obviously the slower he went as one of the opposition the better it was for me.'

Frentzen decided to see for himself if he could settle into F3000 in 1991 and decided, or was advised to decide, to abandon Mercedes and the Junior Team altogether.

Welti remains convinced Frentzen took completely the wrong turn. 'You asked me if he learnt during the 1990 season. Well, he made a huge mistake at the end of this learning period and decided to do only Formula 3000. It was terrible, in terms of the decisions he took, in terms of who he was listening to. I had a talk with him at Donington and I remember driving with him to the airport especially so that I could do that. I told him *just stay with us. That has got to be your future. Do it!* He said *no, no, no, I'm a single-seater driver and that's my designation and that's what I have to do.*'

'He'd been talked into doing F3000 and I thought, how can anyone be that goddamned silly?'

Mass remembers that Frentzen had 'run sporadically' in the Mercedes. 'He did some tests and we wanted him to do more than that but he didn't want to sign a contract because he had already been talked into doing Formula 3000, which he thought was a better way than staying with Mercedes. Had he been joining a top team in 3000 I would have said go for it but the team he signed up for was not a top team. I knew that. I was dumbfounded that he didn't sign a works contract with Mercedes. I talked to him like a sick dog for two hours trying to persuade him and still he wouldn't do it because he had already committed himself – although he couldn't say that. It was one of his weaknesses, that he committed himself so quickly. He made a lot of mistakes which guys do at that sort of stage.'

Elsewhere (*Motoring News*, 1996) Mass has said: 'I despaired when I talked to him to persuade him to drive for Mercedes in 1991 and he didn't want to do it. I couldn't believe his arguments. He was weaving around, and was not straight, because he had committed himself

Balancing act (Gunter Passage).

*He has an easy way with children –
and virtually everybody else too*
(both Gunter Passage).

elsewhere but he couldn't tell us, and I was thinking *how can anybody be so goddamned silly?'*

Neerpasch says: 'There was a problem with Frentzen because, of course, the Juniors developed very well and they were very fast in the first year, 1990. When we did the second year, Frentzen had signed to do a Formula 3000 programme. We had in our contract that Mercedes always got priority date-wise, so if there was a clash he drove the Mercedes. Frentzen had a contract with Camel and a lot of money and he suddenly said *my priority is to go Formula 3000. I'll reach Formula 1 sooner.* The first race of the 1991 season – Suzuka, Japan – we entered him and he didn't appear so we stopped co-operating with him and he went his own way.'

Frentzen says: 'The last two months in the team Mr Sauber could see that I was not really in the right frame of mind, and he felt I was disturbing their ideals. They had many big ideals about the Junior Team but, at that stage, it was not sure for me whether I could get to Formula 1 or not. At the time it was a sports car drive. I knew sports cars were having a difficult time. I thought *I don't want to be a sports car driver, I want to be a Formula 1 driver* and I told them. I had the chance [in 3000] and I had to take it. Peter Sauber was very upset. He didn't say much but he thought I was a bit crazy.'

The team he was joining had been formed in 1975 and, as RAM, contested Formula 1 between 1983 and 1985. They began in Formula 3000 in 1988 as Middlebridge and, in 1990, were known as Superpower. They were based in Bicester and run by John MacDonald, who was experienced enough to have run Alan Jones long before he became F1 World Champion in 1980, and Mick Ralph.

MacDonald remembers that Frentzen had 'advisers at the time and he had Camel money because Camel loved him, so he had the injection which that gave him – meaning the correct amount to do 3000. He was blindingly quick and we targeted him. We'd been in 3000 for some years, we'd run Damon Hill, Mark Blundell and a few other guys so we were well into the 3000 scene. That's that we were doing, 3000.' MacDonald spoke to Frentzen's advisers and said *'why don't you come here? We're a one-car team.'*

The deal was struck but, as MacDonald says, 'unfortunately for Frentzen we picked the wrong car. We went for the Lola and we should have bought a Reynard. Anyway, Camel sponsored us to run him.'

Frentzen's advisers wanted the team to be called Vortex and MacDonald raised no objection to that 'as long as they paid the bills. The name didn't make any difference.

'I'd never met Frentzen before. In fact, I met him initially when we went to Camel in Germany. He was a very quiet guy, a bit reserved I'd say, when you were first introduced to him. Obviously when he became part of the team he lightened up a bit but inwardly he was reserved. We got the car early and we were out running at all the pre-season tests. We had Mugen, which was not a bad engine – overall we had the right package except we ought to have gone for the Reynard.

'Everywhere we went Frentzen was quick: front row at Vallelunga, front row at Pau, always in the top five in qualifying but he could never get the results. Bernie (Ecclestone) used to say to me *when a guy's unlucky he's unlucky forever.* Frentzen was getting the most out of the car and he was the best Lola runner.' That in itself was worthy of note because at the first race, Vallelunga, there were ten Lola runners against eight Reynards and six Ralts. 'The Stewart team were running Marco Apicella and Paul Stewart, they were the works Lola team – in quotation marks – and Frentzen was outqualifying them but he never got the results in the races. He started at the front at Vallelunga and the engine let go after 200 yards . . .'

At Pau, *Autosport* reported that Frentzen briefly had pole and was 'proof of what could be done with the Lola given a huge chunk of commitment. He has great car control and often needs it. He had the definite air of an accident about him though and sure enough . . .'

He went off. 'I braked too late.'

In the race Damon Hill, driving a Lola-Cosworth, made a spectacular start and decided to overtake Frentzen for fifth place on the inside at the first gear Lycee hairpin, a move which did not work. Hill was out immediately but Frentzen pressed on despite the heavy blow to the chassis.

He went off at exactly the point where he had gone off in qualifying.

Next, Jerez. 'We tested there,' MacDonald says, 'a three-day test and he was fastest for three days. We came away thinking *we're going to have this one.* We returned for the race a month later and started twenty eighth! What could possibly have happened in between? We asked ourselves that, all right. In the testing, you see, we'd done full-tank runs, we'd done qualifying runs, we'd done a full race distance and then we go back and – twenty eighth.'

Nor can it have helped that Wendlinger, making his 3000 debut, qualified fifth and finished fifth, Frentzen twelfth. 'That was actually a good run by Heinz-Harald,' MacDonald says, 'getting up from where he started on the grid. But you can't escape the fact that it was still twelfth.'

At Mugello he qualified seventh despite light damage in what was described as a 'scuffle' with Frenchman Paul Belmondo's Reynard. In the race Frentzen was steadily, remorselessly catching McNish for fifth but 'just as H-H was getting close enough to think about having a stab he had a very sideways moment and dropped away' (*Autosport*). He finished sixth.

At Enna he qualified tenth and drove steadily to fifth, setting his fastest lap five laps from the end. Others had had tyre problems but he didn't.

A week before the next round, at Hockenheim, Paul Warwick – who MacDonald had run in British Formula 3 the year before – was killed in a British F3000 race at Oulton Park. Hockenheim qualifying was on

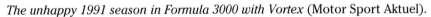

The unhappy 1991 season in Formula 3000 with Vortex (Motor Sport Aktuel).

the Friday, the day of Warwick's funeral in Hampshire. MacDonald and Ralph 'flew from Hockenheim to Paul's funeral and by the time we got back to Hockenheim it was too late.'

This is how it went. MacDonald explains that the team had two cars there, one better than the other. Now listen to *Autosport*: 'There was poor Heinz-Harald Frentzen at his home race, of course, and after one lap of the first session he was parked at the side of the track. With spare cars banned unless the first chassis is damaged beyond repair, the Vortex crew had to find the problem.'

This was compounded by the fact that rain started to fall before the second session, making it almost impossible for the times from the first to be bettered.

The shadow of Alan Jones followed him to Vortex, then on to Williams in 1997

'The sun came out for the second session but not enough to dry the circuit to within five seconds of the pole time. The problem on Frentzen's car was not located anyway.'

MacDonald explains that 'the guy we had left in charge' got it wrong. If he, MacDonald, had been there he'd have put one car firmly in the garage, left it there, concentrated on the other car and 'got Frentzen into the race. As it was he got stranded out on the circuit in heavy rain and didn't make the cut.'

How did Frentzen react to not qualifying at Hockenheim of all places?

In responding, MacDonald uses two of his heroes as benchmarks, one of them Alan Jones. 'If it had been Mike Hailwood or Jones – or even me! – we'd have been rolling round in the pits shouting *what the expletive's happening, what the expletive's going on here?* Frentzen had no real fight, not like Jonesy. I mean, Jonesy was a bastard. He'd have punched everybody out in circumstances like that. I remember me and Jonesy at Mallory Park in a Formula 3000 race squaring up in the pits. I said *you're not expletive trying* and he was out of the car whoosh, and he said to me *come on then, we'll do it now.* That was the de-brief in those days . . .'

This has direct relevance to Frentzen's career because, at Vortex, he was living in the shadow of what Jones had been to MacDonald a decade and a half before. Jones, a rugged Australian, was MacDonald's idea of what a racing driver should really be, and, when he joined Williams in 1978, was also Frank Williams's idea of what a racing driver should really be. The shadow of Jones would follow Frentzen to 1997.

Therefore, a little diversion.

To help you appreciate Jones better, here are a couple of memories from MacDonald.

At Jarama in 1981, when Jones was reigning World Champion with Williams, what MacDonald describes as the 'leper colony' – the small teams – were at the far, far end of the pit lane, a certain Eddie Cheever driving for one of these teams. Something must have taken place out on the track because Jones advanced towards the leper colony. His overalls were undone and the top folded down to his waist, the arms dragging along the ground as he advanced. His face was red and he was murmuring loudly *where's expletive Cheever? Where's expletive Cheever?* 'Anyway, Cheever came out – a big guy and all, Cheever was – and Jones got him by the scruff of the neck. *Get in my expletive way again and I'll expletive drive over the top of you.* Then Jonesy went away, arms still dragging behind him.'

At Zolder that same year something must have taken place out on the track because, MacDonald insists, Nelson Piquet returned to the pits on foot with tears gushing from his eyes and threatening to wreak terrible revenge upon the personage of Jones. Then Jones pulled into the pits and drew up directly in front of where Piquet was standing. Motionless, Jones gave him a stare so full of menace that, far from making towards Jones to whack him, Piquet was *incapable of speech.*

That's the end of the diversion, whose relevance will become clearer in Chapter Five.

The race after Hockenheim in 1991 was Brands Hatch on 18 August where Frentzen qualified twenty-second. *Autosport* reported that 'Frentzen suffered another traumatic day after his non-qualification at Hockenheim. He chose the fifth gear Hawthorn Bend to have a spin, going gearbox-first into the tyres and knocking himself out in the process. The Vortex Lola was not sufficiently harmed to allow use of the spare, so H-H had to press on with his repaired car in the afternoon. He thought it felt odd and suspected he may have cracked the gearbox.' He finished the race twelfth.

It brings us to the next round at Spa and a weekend full of heaviest irony. The Formula 3000 race would be part of the Belgian Grand Prix programme, run on the Saturday. Every aspect of the weekend would emphasise that Frentzen had taken a wrong turn.

Jordan, now in Formula 1, had a vacancy because their driver Bertrand Gachot was in prison after a dispute with a London taxi driver. Eddie Jordan had his eye on Schumacher to replace Gachot, partnering Andrea de Cesaris. Jordan had watched Schumacher in the Mercedes sports car at the Nurburgring on 18 August (while Frentzen slogged round Brands Hatch towards that twelfth place). The Schumacher/Wendlinger car was up to fifth early on but the engine let go after ten laps. Not that that mattered. Jordan signed Schumacher for the Belgian Grand Prix.

However 'the plan was still to develop Michael and Wendlinger for Mercedes in Formula 1,' Jochen Neerpasch says. 'When Michael went to that race at Spa with Jordan it was we – Mercedes – who drew up the contract. It had an option for him to continue with Jordan but also an option to get him back as soon as Mercedes were ready for Formula 1.'

Trevor Foster is in a position to compare Frentzen and Schumacher but before he does that here significantly is his memory of Schumacher arriving at Jordan. 'You can see if a driver has *it* or not in 20 laps. I said to Eddie Jordan: you can take a driver from Formula 3 or Formula 3000, put him in a Formula 1 car and within the 20 laps you'll know whether he is having to use 100% of his mental capacity to keep the thing on the road or whether he takes it all in his stride and you realise he is using 80% and the other 20% is *thinking*. Michael first tested for us at Silverstone and within five laps the brakes were glowing, he was flicking it through the little chicane on the South circuit totally at ease. In those days we had very little money and the car was his race car for Spa with a brand new engine in it. We didn't want any damage so I brought him in and – it sounds a joke now, doesn't it? – I said *listen, calm down, take it easy*. He said *what's the problem? I don't understand. I'm in control*.'

On the Friday at Spa, while Frentzen was qualifying a respectable seventh for the 3000 race, Schumacher was stirring the whole of Grand Prix racing by going eighth fastest in the first qualifying session for the Grand Prix – faster than Piquet, for instance. Foster remembers him

Right *The tyre choice that went wrong at Monaco.*

'sitting in his car and I said to him *Michael, you're sure you're not pushing too hard?* and he said calmly *no, I'm on the limit but I'm not over the limit*. Believe it or not, there were a couple of places where Andrea was quicker than him. So what did Schumacher do? That night he overlaid the laps [detailed print-outs], looked at how he was taking the corners. The next day – boof.'

That was the Saturday, Schumacher taking care of those places where de Cesaris had been quicker. It helped him go an astonishing sixth quickest in second qualifying – translating to the fourth row of the grid, with only Senna, Alain Prost, Nigel Mansell, Gerhard Berger, Jean Alesi and Piquet in front of him. Later that afternoon Frentzen moved to fifth place in the 3000 race: not very good, not very bad, not really very much at all.

'Frentzen was quicker, but Michael has moved on, developed the whole package'

Autosport reported that Frentzen 'made some progress' when a driver called Fabrizio Giovanardi 'got the first part of the Bus Stop all wrong. Frentzen flicked alongside and braved it out into the second part. He got away with it and soon glued himself to Eric Helary's gearbox. Frentzen is a driver who is tremendous to watch. He has uncanny car control and very often needs it.'

I venture to Foster that Frentzen has had to live virtually all of his career in Schumacher's deep shadow and it's arguably worse than that because the received wisdom is that once upon a time Frentzen was faster than Schumacher; hence the view that Frentzen was the one to take Schumacher on in Formula 1, and that's a hell of a task.

'Well, it is really. There's a similarity between Frentzen and Mika Hakkinen. If you remember, Hakkinen and Schumacher came together [literally] at Macau in 1990 when Michael was leading and Hakkinen tried to overtake him. Hakkinen retired and Michael won. If you further remember, earlier that year Hakkinen went over to a round of the German Formula 3 and paralysed them all, including Michael.' In other words, Schumacher had worked on the problem of being as quick as Hakkinen and solved it.

'People can say to Frentzen *well, you were quicker than Michael and* people can point to that time at Hockenheim when Hakkinen was quicker – but they're not now. Why? Because Michael has moved on. As a driver, Heinz-Harald finds it very difficult to work on the rest of the package – apart from the driving – to make himself special, to make himself complete. Driving the car at high speed, lots of car control, sliding it around: that comes totally naturally to him. The rest of it is totally alien. That's what he struggles with and that's where Schumacher has left him.'

While Frentzen prepared himself for the round after Spa – at Le Mans on 22 September – Schumacher stirred Grand Prix racing further, and did so inadvertently.

Neerpasch explains that 'for Spa we paid for Michael to drive for Jordan.' The two parties – Neerpasch/Mercedes and Jordan – reportedly fell out over the amount of advertising space on the car and 'we changed to Benetton, but also with a clause in the contract that as soon as Mercedes were ready for Formula 1 we would get him back. In other words, we at Mercedes wanted to train our drivers in a professional and methodical way, which normally drivers never get. The whole Formula 1 world was very astonished when Schumacher did what he did at Spa. *Where did this Schumacher come from?* people were asking because they didn't realise what had been happening. Not only did nobody know Schumacher before Spa, nobody knew what the Juniors had been doing. Nobody realised.

'Later on, when Frentzen saw the development of Schumacher and Wendlinger, he realised he had made a mistake. He knows this now.' That said, Neerpasch assesses Frentzen as a 'very sympathetic man, a really nice man.'

At Le Mans he qualified twenty second, another paradox because in earlier testing he had been second quickest. In the race, while those who knew Frentzen savoured the prospect of a spectacular charge, he tangled with Hill again, continued (again) and eventually went off (again).

At Nogaro, the final round, he qualified ninth. *Motoring News* described how he 'bullied' the car, 'spinning a couple of times en route to a one minute 18.53 seconds. "We lowered the car a little in the afternoon, which improved things," he said. Like [Frenchman Laurent] Aiello he was terrific to watch unless you were either of faint heart or part of the team management.' In the race the wishbone broke after 22 laps.

Left *Beaulieu Motor Museum, but strictly amongst the living* (ICN U.K. Bureau).

That week, the Leyton House Formula 1 team announced they had signed Wendlinger to drive the last two Grands Prix of the season. At the time Neerpasch said: 'You must take your opportunities when they come. Both Karl and Michael continue to be Mercedes drivers. We release them for Formula 1 but if the time comes we are able to have them back.'

One report said that 'as Mercedes did' when Schumacher drove for Jordan at Spa, they would 'bankroll' Wendlinger and try to recoup the money by selling sponsorship on the car and Wendlinger's overalls.

It meant Schumacher was firmly in Formula 1, Wendlinger had reached Formula 1 and Frentzen was nowhere. Max Welti of Sauber summarises it neatly. 'The ironical thing is that Michael stayed and got into the Jordan, although he was helped, of course. Michael is a straightforward thinker. There are no ifs and buts, he's just learning, learning, learning, learning like hell – and he doesn't forget things.'

Reflecting, John MacDonald gazes at the Formula 3000 Championship table of 1991 and says 'unlucky driver? I mean, fourteenth with five points. He was better than that! Oh yes, he was better than that, a quick driver, big balls.'

What is this speed?

'These special drivers have no fear. They are committed to the fast lap in qualifying: *you put the tyres on, I'll do the time*. Frentzen is quick, Frentzen is quicker than Schumacher – I said that at the time – but he hasn't got that aspect which Schumacher has. Schumacher is like a dog, sinks his teeth in and will not let go. If the car isn't any good Schumacher won't be fobbed off, he'll be on to you – *get the damned car right* – and he'll go on and on all night until he's got it. He'd be hanging on to you all night! Frentzen can be washed aside a little bit, you know. There was no question of him staying with us another year because Camel withdrew the money.'

Adam Cooper, a journalist close to the situation, wrote that at the end of 1991 Frentzen was 'out in the cold.' His career perished in the face of the impression Schumacher had made with Benetton, and Camel Germany 'abruptly switched its attention to the new superstar.' It left, Cooper concluded, Frentzen with nothing; and while Schumacher confirmed the initial impression he'd made in Formula 1 by scoring points regularly in 1992 Frentzen, without any drive, had 'all but given up on the sport. He seemed set for a career in the family undertaking business.'

'I missed the chance to be a super talent,' Frentzen has said. 'The two years in Formula 3000 were a mess for me and my image. I had nothing to do any more: I was at home at the start of 1992 concentrating on something which had nothing to do with motor racing – becoming a taxi driver perhaps! I had no chance in racing. I couldn't even get a drive in German saloon cars and if I couldn't get a ride there then Formula 1 wasn't looking good.

'He improved a lot with us – each step we explained everything to him about the car'

'I think I have learned to be a professional race driver [Frentzen was speaking in 1994]. I never had the opportunity in Formula 3000, where I always felt I was under pressure. That first year with Eddie Jordan was too much for me. I didn't have the experience to set up the car properly and I was not really in the mind to handle it. In the second year I had the attitude to give my best but it was impossible to prove anything when the car is no good, you are under pressure from race to race and you know that you have a gun at your neck.'

That gun, we may surmise, was vindicating the decision to leave Mercedes.

Frentzen did secure a drive at the Le Mans 24 Hour sports car race in mid-June, however. It was with Shunji Kasuya and Mideshi Matsuda in the Lola Judd which they qualified twelfth. *Autosport's* thumbnail sketch of the race is perfect: 'Frentzen qualified 12th with lap of 3m 40.207s on Friday. Ninth after one hour. Gearbox problems after four hours. 'Box changed after seven hours. Frentzen set several fastest laps during the early hours. Eleventh, 27 laps down, after 12 hours. Two accidents in Kasuya's hands, requiring long front-end rebuilds. New windscreen and nose at 6 a.m. [Dutchman Charles] Zwolsman transferred himself into car so Matsuda didn't drive. Finished 13th.'

Then, when all seemed lost, the unlucky driver got lucky. A German driver, Volker Weidler, was racing Formula 3000 in Japan with a leading team there, Nova. Weidler began to suffer from tinnitus, a ringing in the ears, and stopped racing. As his replacement Weidler recommended Frentzen.

He contested the last three rounds – one at Fuji, two at Suzuka – and finished the final round third. It was, reportedly, a well-judged performance despite the fact that he had difficulty adjusting to Japanese tyres, of which more in a moment. He took five points from these three rounds, making him fourteenth in the Championship (astonishingly, just what he had done with Vortex over the whole European F3000 season).

As if to emphasise the luck, MacDonald says that 'Frentzen didn't go to Japan straight away, did he? He only got the ride when that other German kid, Weidler, had ear problems.'

It is a great, reverberating and eternal truth about motor racing that how you arrive somewhere is infinitely less important than what you do when you get there. Whole careers have been built upon chance – like, in 1981, Alan Jones telling Frank Williams he was retiring and telling him so late in the season that all the leading drivers had already signed or re-signed elsewhere. Williams looked around and could only find a driver who, in four seasons of flogging round in uncompetitive cars, had taken a third place and a fifth place. That was Keke Rosberg. He became World Champion with Williams the following year.

Ironically, perhaps, in 1992 Mercedes abandoned their strategy of going into Formula 1 – at any rate, by forming their own team. Neerpasch explains that 'Sauber, together with Mercedes, still had the contracts to have the drivers and then Mercedes lost those drivers. Two weeks before the announcement should have been made – that Mercedes were entering Formula 1 with the Silver Arrows – the company, in a deep recession, had to get rid of 27,000 people and they thought they couldn't do both: get rid of the people and spend money on Formula 1. So they decided to cancel Formula 1. This was the reason I left Mercedes although, in all these decisions, you can understand the different points of view.' Sauber did enter Formula 1 in 1993 but with the enigmatic logo *concept by Mercedes-Benz* along its flank.

Frentzen stayed in Japan in 1993 for a full season of All-Japan Formula 3000 with Nova, whose experienced engineer, Moto Moriwaki, says Frentzen 'had very good natural talent but he was technically naive. He improved a lot with us. Each step, we explained everything to him about the car, because basically he could drive it pretty well no matter how it was set up.

'He's not the most complete driver I've ever worked with but he's one of the fastest, though my outstanding memory is actually one of sadness. There was a very wet race at Mine. He was tremendous, around 3.5 seconds quicker than anyone else on the circuit. Mauro Martini, his team-mate, was second a long way behind. Then, with 20 of the 80 laps remaining, his oil pressure dropped and his engine seized. He'd been driving so well, mature and controlled.'

Frentzen completed the season ninth in the Championship with eight points (compared to, say, Irvine, joint first with 32). It prompts a hard evaluation from John MacDonald: 'Frentzen didn't do any good in Japan. Irvine went there and did do well, but Irvine's strong, he's another one who when he bites you he ain't gonna let go . . .'

MacDonald's view is not shared by everyone and anyway there were consolations. He was chosen for a Bridgestone-Mugen test drive. Bridgestone were working on race tyres which (in 1997) would be used in Formula 1; Mugen were of course a Honda close relative; and Tyrrell provided the car.

'The first time I drove a Formula 1 car,' Frentzen says, 'was 12 May, nobody around to share it with me. I was thinking it's not such a big thing, you know. It wasn't that much quicker than an F3000 car. I was driving a Formula 1 car without the pressure of everyone watching to see if I was quick or not. You just drive, they ask you how it feels – and you get paid for that?'

Kees van de Grint went to Japan that year because of his work with Bridgestone and watched Frentzen – who was a Bridgestone runner – with particular interest although he wasn't at that first Formula 1 test. 'I must say he had changed completely. That is what had happened during his time in Japan. I know he found it difficult to use the qualifying tyres but he was a much, much better race driver: he had improved his weak points enormously. The Bridgestone test driver used to be Volker Wiedler but he got the ear illness, his replacement was Martini and then, for whatever reason Martini couldn't do a test and just because Frentzen was in the same team they took him. The Japanese were very impressed with his testing ability and from then on he became the test driver.'

Of his 1993 season *Autosport* wrote: 'For Nova Engineering twins Frentzen and '92 champion Mauro Martini, it was a year to forget. Saddled with the T93/50 and works Mugen engines which were not up to scratch, Martini knew from the outset that he would not be able to defend his title although he won in the rain at Mine. That victory should have gone to Frentzen. He was sensational in the wet, miles quicker than anyone else, until his engine failed. Elsewhere there were flashes of brilliance but few hard results. However he never gave less than 100% and was always on the ragged edge.'

The evaluation of Neerpasch: 'He had to go to Japan and he lost two years. At that time he wanted to be the first of the Juniors into Formula 1 – which is normal, oh sure – but he lost the two years.'

The evaluation of McNish: 'He had a difficult situation in 1992. He was out of a drive, a similar situation to myself at times, and went to Japan. I think the culture helped: the fact that there was a bit of pressure off, the way things worked out there. He was able, slowly, to rebuild his confidence and don't forget he was with Nova. He

It was time for Peter Sauber to have a little chat with Heinz-Harald Frentzen about the future (Gunter Passage).

developed and he learnt to calm down, harness the speed and not crash – because you can't crash.'

The evaluation of Welti: 'What Frentzen didn't lose during this period of the very difficult time was his speed. Life was so hard with him at that time that it really calmed him down.'

In what sense?

'A lot of people forgot him completely during those bad years, and there weren't just a lot but loads of people who stopped believing in him anymore. In fact almost nobody did still believe in him. From the point of view of his morale that must have been an extremely tough time. He appeared in Europe for some sports car races and I remember meeting him at Le Mans where he was so fast, so unbelievably fast in an uncompetitive car. During the night and in the rain he constantly drove the fastest laps. He was really impressive at Le Mans, I have to say. Peter obviously saw that as well. Peter decided: *look, he's quick and been through the difficult time.*'

Peter was Peter Sauber whose team was deep into its debut Formula 1 season, with Wendlinger and JJ Lehto. They'd finish with 12 points (Wendlinger 7, Lehto 5), joint sixth place in the Constructors' table and not perhaps what Peter Sauber had had in mind. Wendlinger would be staying but Lehto wouldn't.

It was time to have a word with Heinz-Harald Frentzen about how he saw his future. It was time to bring the boy home, which is how early one morning he heard his phone ringing, picked it up and, through jet-lag, heard a voice saying *it's Sauber here.*

• CHAPTER FOUR •

The believer

MAX WELTI, SAUBER team director, tells the tale. 'Peter Sauber said *I'm in trouble with drivers, there is really nobody on the marker anymore, we are a young Formula 1 team and nobody's interested in us – so let's try it with Heinz-Harald.* He knew it was a risk in terms of him not having Grand Prix experience. Heinz-Harald was very quick from the beginning but obviously he did lack experience, which is nothing but normal.'

Frentzen had had no connection with Sauber from his leaving until late 1992 when Mercedes were holding an official reception and asked him along. 'I was invited – strangely,' Frentzen says. 'I didn't know what to do there! I met Mr Sauber and he said *you see what you lost*, because by then the Formula 1 cars were testing and setting good times. I said *yes, congratulations, it's a very nice car* and went back to Japan.'

Peter Sauber, however, was curious and on one of Frentzen's trips to Europe arranged for him to have a test in this nice car.

Frentzen remembers that 'immediately I felt 100 per cent at home in it. I was lucky because I was well trained after all the testing in Japan. I was immediately quick, I think I was so quick Mr Sauber didn't believe it! The idea grew more and more but I'm not sure he was 100 per cent convinced because many people were saying *I don't think Frentzen is right.*'

On 12 October 1993 Frentzen's telephone rang.

'I'd just come back from Japan and I was lying in bed feeling jet-lagged. Sauber rang at eight in the morning and said *yes, we're going to choose you.* I said *yeah.* Then I held the phone away from my face, shouted *YeeeaAAHHH* and put it back to my ear. It was only under the

97

shower that I fully realised what was happening. It was unbelievable – I had a Formula 1 drive. It sounded like a novel. I didn't believe that anything like this, my second chance, could really happen.'

He tested the new Sauber, the C13, in Estoril in early February 1994, settling to a rhythm (after a spin) and working prudently down to laps of one minute 12 seconds, a highly respectable time. Wendlinger was there and consistently a second and a half slower although for a reason. Mario Illien of Ilmor Engineering, working in conjunction with Mercedes on the engines, said: 'Heinz-Harald went very well and we had no dramas of any sort. It was an essentially positive test for us. The two cars were different. Heinz-Harald worked on aerodynamics during the three days while Karl concentrated on the mechanical package, spring, shock absorbers, that sort of thing. They left the aerodynamics entirely alone on his car and he never got to try Heinz-Harald's package so you can't really compare their lap times.'

A more significant test was at Imola in March. Schumacher was quickest (1m 21.078s), Senna, now with Williams, next (1m 21.244s), Frentzen seventh (1m 23.378s) – but Wendlinger sixth (1m 23.346s). We are talking about small differences but they magnify themselves in Grand Prix racing because, in layman's terms, the performance of the cars and drivers are generally very, very close. The span of the times above from Schumacher to Frentzen represent an eyeblink after the three miles of Imola. The naturally gifted drivers like Frentzen can find fractions in any Grand Prix car and if these fractions are not literally priceless they come expensive. Ask any team owner who's had to pay the driver who finds them.

This is the story of one man's first season in the right place for some of the right and some of the wrong reasons with, for context, what his team-mates Wendlinger, de Cesaris and Lehto were doing in the most direct comparison.

Consider first qualifying for the debut in Brazil where, on a track measuring 4.325 kilometres, 11 drivers did laps of one minute 18 seconds. Hakkinen (McLaren) produced one minute 18.122 which put him on the third row of the provisional grid, Frentzen (1:18.144) alongside. Another context, here. New technical regulations limited technology to try to bring the front and back of the grid closer, and less than two seconds covered numbers 3 to 17 on the grid. Next day he improved to fifth – confident and impressive, as one report said.

'I felt a little nervous on Friday morning and decided to start cautiously. Am I really fifth on the grid? I still can't believe it. When I saw the clouds getting darker and darker I decided to use the second set of tyres early, which was the right decision. Towards the end of the session I went out on rain tyres, important to me because during all our winter testing I've never had the opportunity to run on Goodyear rain tyres.'

Peter Sauber estimated 'this is one of the best debuts of a Formula 1 driver for a long time.'

At the green light Senna led, Frentzen keeping out of trouble in the jostle to the first corner. He settled into fifth in front of Hakkinen, who began to pressure. Early movement: Hakkinen went by and Frentzen ran a comfortable sixth, fifth when Hakkinen retired on lap 14 – the electrics failed. Frentzen retired a couple of laps later. He'd looked solid until then, despite a drinks tube leaking into his visor, and insisted he'd been concentrating on getting to the finish, no heroics. 'I'm obviously very disappointed. Suddenly I lost the rear end of the car over a rise. What a shame. This was really unnecessary.'

1994, first year in Formula 1, first of the three Sauber years (ICN U.K. Bureau).

At the Pacific at Aida, Japan, he started from the sixth row (Wendlinger the tenth) and ran eighth despite a touch of cramp in his left shoulder, kept on solidly and finished fifth. 'I'm very happy not only for the result and the two points but because I drove a good race. Right after the start I had a difficult moment when Senna spun in front of me and I had to avoid him. Afterwards I found a good pace, trying

France, and Frentzen leads both McLarens on the first lap (ICN U.K. Bureau).

not to use the tyres too much. Towards the end I heard a strange noise from the engine so I slowed down a little. There was a big gap behind me and I didn't risk losing position.'

And to Imola. Roland Ratzenberger (Simtek) died when he crashed 18 minutes into the Saturday qualifying session and Frentzen, sixth fastest the day before, took no part. Frentzen uttered three sentences: 'Roland was a friend of mine. We had a good time together in Japan. This is a very sad day for me.'

Frentzen related to a local Moenchengladbach photographer, Gunter Passage, how Ratzenberger once saved his life and Passage related the tale to me. 'They were driving in 3000 in Japan and stayed in the same hotel in Tokyo. They went out for dinner or a beer and met some Japanese girls.' There followed some dispute with a couple of men over the girls, and one of the men 'came with a big knife behind Heinz-Harald and was going to kill him. Ratzenberger grabbed the man by the wrist' and prevented the knife attack. Frentzen said that Ratzenberger 'was my best friend.' (Frentzen's father would go to the place where Ratzenberger crashed to pay his own respects, see page 135.)

The San Marino Grand Prix remains a culmination, an ending, a terrible conclusion, Senna mortally wounded against the wall at the Tamburello corner. Frentzen finished seventh. 'This was a very, very sad weekend and it is difficult for me to give any comments. At the first start I could hardly avoid JJ Lehto who stalled on the grid, and at the second start to the formation lap I stalled the engine myself. Then I damaged the nose of my car when Blundell closed the door on me. Even during the race I had to think of my friend Roland who died yesterday. It was terrible.'

Peter Sauber struggled, as everyone else struggled, amidst the wreckage of the Grand Prix meeting. 'This was a black weekend and I'm almost unable to say something about it. We have to make a lot of thoughts about all the accidents. On the one hand I'm pleased with the performance of our team, on the other hand I must say that this has no importance in comparison to what happened in these three days.'

The Imola aftermath is well charted: the Wendlinger crash at Monaco two weeks later: an innocent seeming moment during Thursday free practice, the car into the Armco, Wendlinger in a Nice hospital in a coma. Sauber withdrew from the Grand Prix.

One of the most delicate and difficult aspects of motor racing is that it does continue despite injuries and fatalities, although this is not the place to explore that. What is clear is that Sauber would return at the race after Monaco – Spain – and that the Williams team needed a driver. They thought of Frentzen.

'Frank did actually offer him a drive in 1994 and Frentzen turned it down for loyalty,' Welti says. 'Heinz-Harald knew that without Peter Sauber he wouldn't ever have been in Formula 1. I also think he never regretted turning Williams down. He believed in the Sauber team, he believed he would be able to grow with the team and the team would be able to grow with him – which did take place up to a certain extent.'

What is astonishing is that, on the strength of only three races, Frank Williams considered Frentzen good enough to handle a car which could win Championships.

'The offer constituted the happiest moment of my life,' Frentzen says, 'not only because Williams asked me but also because it was to replace the man who was my idol from the day I started karting. But I could not leave Sauber. It would not have been the honourable thing to do. On the one hand I was telling myself that I could be in a top team, and on the other I felt that I had no right to be there.'

Sauber ran only Frentzen in Spain, where he was fifth when the gearbox failed after 21 laps. In Canada, where the experienced de Cesaris joined Sauber, he retired after five laps, accident; but in France he went to the end, fourth. In Britain he finished seventh although he found Silverstone 'quite a difficult track to learn. I was lucky in the morning session before first qualifying when I followed Michael Schumacher, and then I watched him during qualifying on TV . . . well,

Wendlinger, so badly hurt at Monaco, is here at the Italian Grand Prix flanked by Johnny Herbert (left) and JJ Lehto (ICN U.K. Bureau).

I know all the German journalists like a good story! Seriously, I did improve on a couple of corners, although it was a risk to try his line in qualifying.'

In Germany he was an innocent victim of an extensive crash. 'My start was good but at the entrance to the first corner Hakkinen suddenly pulled from the right to the left and went sideways. Several cars tried to avoid him but there wasn't enough space. Finally Blundell hit me at the right front wheel and I went into the gravel. There was nothing I could do. I managed to continue but I had a flat tyre and the suspension was bent so I was forced to stop.'

In Hungary he retired after 39 laps with a gearbox problem, and in Belgium qualified on the fifth row. The fast times were set in first qualifying, a session which began wet but ultimately offered a tantalising chance in the dry which Rubens Barrichello (Jordan) took for provisional pole. 'I decided to stay out on wet tyres,' Frentzen explained, 'and about three laps from the end I saw Barrichello on slicks and thought *ummm* but my tactics were right – it was just that I didn't have enough experience on wet tyres, and mine probably weren't at their best by the end anyway.'

In the race Frentzen pressured Barrichello and pressured him so hard that he, Frentzen, spun. It happens. 'Barrichello tried everything to defend himself but I must say he was always fair. I was praying I could overtake him because I was sure I could pull away once I was past but I pushed too hard. After the spin I had reverse but no first, second or third gears and I didn't know where they had gone.'

In Italy he retired after 22 laps, an engine problem, after a crash in qualifying – de Cesaris was outqualifying him (and did, fourth row against Frentzen's sixth). 'The car understeered too much there and I tried to correct it by pumping the throttle. Unfortunately the back stepped out and I crashed.'

Of second qualifying in Portugal he said, 'I think that was one of my best laps [one minute 21.921 seconds, worth the fifth row] since I came into Formula 1. We managed to improve the car in free practice so it was perfectly balanced.' He retired after 31 laps with a transmission problem. And it got better.

At the European Grand Prix, at Jerez, he held provisional pole for a long time and qualified on the second row – a Sauber hadn't been that high before. Of that lap and the incessant search for fractions he said that 'on my first run I braked a little late for one corner and on the second run there was oil in the hairpin.' He finished the race sixth and told the tale himself. 'Mansell had too much wheelspin at the start so I was able to pass him before the first corner. After that I tried to save the tyres because my strategy was to stop only once. I was under pressure from Mansell and Barrichello but it was no problem to keep them under control – the car handled very well despite the fuel load. My pit stop was very good but on the second set of tyres the car understeered and that cost me time. Although I hoped for more before the race, I am satisfied having scored one point. In the end I had to fight hard to finish in front of Katayama, who attacked at his maximum. I'm exhausted because physically I didn't feel a hundred per cent well all weekend.'.

In Japan he qualified on the second row. 'I have a good mental feeling on this circuit because I know many things here and I just had to put it all together. The car was brilliant.' He finished the race sixth.

With the experienced Andrea de Cesaris in 1994 (ICN U.K. Bureau).

At this point McLaren and Mercedes announced a five-year deal which would begin in 1995. It meant Mercedes were severing their connection with Sauber. Jurgen Huppert, a member of the Mercedes board, said: 'In Formula 1, Mercedes is on a good path but we have not yet received the results we wanted. These problems are not all Sauber's fault. The technical changes after the San Marino Grand Prix didn't help and neither did Wendlinger's injury. However, we have always said we won't finance a team but instead be in partnership with them. This is why we didn't bring back the Silver Arrows, although the decision not to was an emotional one. We had to assist Peter Sauber financially and with his self-financing not looking in line for 1995 we had to terminate our deal.'

In Australia he had understeer during the race 'and I was under much pressure from Blundell. That forced me to get everything out of the car

Argentina, almost solitude, 1995 (Ford).

I could until he stopped' – an intriguing way of putting it. Blundell explains: 'I was quicker than Frentzen but I couldn't get by and Alesi was catching me. I showed Frentzen I was going to overtake at the hairpin four or five times but he decided to turn in on me when I made my move and he hit my sidepod.'

Nor did Frentzen's anxieties end there. Berger led and was coming along to lap him. Both decorum and the rules insist that the slower driver allows the faster driver unhindered rites of passage. 'I'm really sorry for him because he got stuck behind me. On my [pit] board I saw that Alesi was catching me and I only realised it was Gerhard who wanted to lap me when he showed me the fist. I then reacted too much which allowed Alesi to overtake me as well.' He finished seventh.

Sauber got the Ford Zetec engine and, despite the usual optimistic noises when the deal was announced, it was not competitive with Renault, Ferrari or Mercedes.

In mid-January 1995, Frentzen made the obligatory optimistic noises.

'I have to say it was a very good relationship with Mercedes last year and to be honest I haven't met the people from Ford – the specialists – yet, but I know Ford has had a lot of success in Formula 1 engines and has a lot of experience. I'm really looking forward to joining with them, to working together, to seeing what they do.'

Frentzen gave the C14 with the Ford engine its first run at Paul Ricard in early February, Wendlinger drove it too, and the car covered 115 laps without problems. Then the team headed for more testing at Estoril. Bad weather – and a crash by Frentzen, spinning on what was assumed to be oil – made this test unsatisfactory. It did inevitably provide direct comparisons, however. Some early times:

Hill (Williams-Renault)	1m 22.53s
Alesi (Ferrari)	1m 24.76s
Frentzen (Sauber-Ford)	1m 24.76s
Hakkinen (McLaren Mercedes)	1m 26.00s
Wendlinger (Sauber-Ford)	1m 26.27s

Testing can be deceptive, in the sense that you don't always know who's trying to achieve what but instinctively they all like to come away having seen what the car will really do, even for a few hot laps; and remember how small fractions magnify themselves. The gap Hill-to-Frentzen was, in Formula 1 measurements, a very big one indeed.

As the testing continued, Hill got down to 1m 21.77, Alesi to 1m 22.29 while David Coulthard (Williams), Berger (Ferrari), Schumacher (Benetton-Renault), Ukyo Katayama (Tyrrell-Yamaha) and Hakkinen were all quicker than Frentzen. The testing culminated with Schumacher quickest (1m 21.30s).

This is the story of one man's second season in the right place for some of the right and some of the wrong reasons with, for comparison, what Wendlinger and then Jean-Christophe Boullion were doing. This is included because Wendlinger was regarded as potentially a leading driver one day and Boullion a fine prospect. The comparison serves to illuminate how good Frentzen was becoming.

At Interlagos for the Brazilian Grand Prix, he qualified on the seventh row – regarded as a disappointment – and retired after ten laps when the electrics failed. Wendlinger qualified on the tenth row and also retired.

For the Argentine Grand Prix, he qualified on the fifth row. *Motoring*

News reported that 'without any points from Brazil, Peter Sauber arrived in Buenos Aires with new winglets in his hand luggage. As well as going back into the wind tunnel between races, the team had worked on the car's damping. Heinz-Harald Frentzen's enthusiasm was anything but dampened, and there was little doubt that his tenure of third place at the end of the opening day owed more to his brilliance than it did to the C14's. Second in timed practice, he dropped only one slot in the afternoon – this, after calmly radioing in to inform the engineers that a 360 degree spin had 'warmed the tyres.' The performance must have warmed Sauber, too, although, unable to find a balance of Saturday, the German dropped three rows in as many minutes.'

Wendlinger, who'd qualified on the eleventh row, confessed: 'I have to say the difference between me and Heinz-Harald is mainly down to the driving.'

In the race Frentzen finished fifth but two laps behind the winner, Hill. Wendlinger was out at the start after a collision with Bertrand Gachot (Pacific).

Testing at Estoril – testing how many people can walk across the gravel trap (Gunter Passage).

Between Argentina and San Marino, Sauber altered the design of the C14 to a high nose configuration. The handling had been so bad in Argentina that Frentzen felt the only time the car's balance was right was when it had full fuel tanks. At San Marino he qualified on the seventh row (Wendlinger the eleventh again) but the car didn't seem much better: persistent understeer. In the race he finished sixth and said that 'scoring a point at the end of a difficult weekend was satisfactory.'

In Spain he qualified on the sixth row (Wendlinger the tenth). 'Although I expected a big improvement I was having to fight really hard each lap just to pick up tenths of a second.' In the race his tyres quickly lost grip. 'I had a fright when I came into the pit lane, looked at the dashboard readout and saw I was doing 129kph in the 120kph limit. It was only later that I discovered that the dashboard readout was stuck at 129kph!'

Before Monaco, Wendlinger was replaced by Boullion, a 26-year-old Frenchman presently employed as the Williams test driver. The simple truth was that Wendlinger could not compete with the times Frentzen had been setting.

'There are two different stories,' Wendlinger says of his time at Sauber. 'You can take the era before my accident, when I think I was quick enough and we were doing more or less the same times. Take the first Grand Prix of 1994, Interlagos. It was 500ths of a second between us in qualifying [Frentzen 1m 17.806s, Wendlinger 1m 17.927s] and at Imola it was close too [Frentzen 1m 23.119s, Wendlinger 1m 23.347s]. So we were on virtually the same level from the point of view of speed and everything. And the relationship between us was OK, it was no problem. We worked together quite normally, although what can you really say about team work? There is team work of course but the important thing and the important person for you is your race engineer. He's the guy you have to work with, and the set up of the two cars in a team is never the same anyway.'

Then you had the accident at Monaco in 1994.

'After the accident the relationship was still OK between us and no risk of it being destroyed, because he was the number one driver in the team and there was a big gap to me. He was quicker, so no fight against each other, no bad politics, nothing.'

Before the accident you were as quick, afterwards you weren't.

'It was partly because of the accident and partly because of something else. If you have such a big injury it is difficult to be mentally on the highest level. There was a test at Barcelona. They said to me OK, *you want to have a contract for 1995, you have to do the same times as Frentzen.* I said *impossible after six months of rest.* They said *this is Formula 1.* I did go as quick as Frentzen – but there were other tests when I was slower. This was the mental part which was going up and down in my head.

'The next problem was that in 1995 the car was over-weight and my personal weight was 16 or 17 kilos more than Frentzen. So that, with a little bit from the car, meant I was driving with 20 kilos more than him. At some circuits this represented seven tenths of a second a lap, maybe more than a second. When you make the addition from this – the disadvantage from the weight and, like I said, from my mental side – the sum was that I was just too slow.'

At Monaco Frentzen qualified on the seventh row (Boullion the tenth) and in the race finished sixth, which was two laps behind the winner, Schumacher. Boullion was classified eighth.

The rumour that a leading team like McLaren might want Frentzen seemed entirely plausible

---

In Canada strong rumours circulated suggesting he'd replace Blundell at McLaren, who of course had Mercedes engines. Frentzen denied these rumours, saying 'I know only as much as you know from the newspapers. Of course I have a good relationship with Mercedes and talking about the future is no problem but at the moment I am completely a Sauber driver.' Formula 1 abounds in rumours and most of them never come true but paradoxically they are an indication of a driver's stature. That a leading team like McLaren might want Frentzen seemed entirely plausible. In qualifying he was going markedly faster in the second session than the first when he was forced to abort a flying lap because Irvine spun. Never mind. 'I thought I would be even quicker on my next lap but I had traffic problems.' He was on the sixth row (Boullion the ninth) and in the race the engine failed after 26 laps (Boullion spun off after 19).

In France he qualified on the sixth row (Boullion the eighth) and estimated that 'all things considered, it was good' to have improved in the second session: from one minute 21.111s on the Friday to one

Corinna, once Frentzen's girlfriend, now Mrs Michael Schumacher (ATP).

Tanja, the girlfriend (Formula One Pictures).

minute 20.309s. In the race he finished tenth, a lap behind the winner, Schumacher (Boullion out with a transmission problem).

How a driver copes with frustration is important, sometimes crucial, and mid-season 1995 was a test of that. In Britain he qualified on the sixth row (Boullion the eighth) and for once allowed the frustration to show. 'I would tell you what is wrong but there isn't enough time left in the day.' In the race he finished sixth (Boullion ninth). In Germany he qualified – it was becoming habitual – on the sixth row (Boullion the seventh) and in the race retired after 32 laps, an engine problem (Boullion fifth). Cryptically Frentzen said 'I cannot think of any other racetrack where you are hard on the throttle for so long that it eventually makes your right foot numb.'

In Hungary he qualified – of course – on the sixth row (Boullion the tenth) after another abort, this time when he came upon Andrea Montermini's slow-moving Pacific. Up to that point it had been Frentzen's best lap. Angry, Frentzen tried again but by now the tyres had lost maximum adhesion. He was – of course – pushing and went off into a gravel trap. In the race he finished fifth (Boullion tenth) and one report said that 'ironically Frentzen's balance had actually improved once his Sauber lost its rear wing gurney flap near the end. [A gurney flap is an addition to the rear wing, normally set at 90 degrees.] Nursing a stiff neck, and still weak from recent illness, he finished two tenths of a second away from Herbert, who was fourth.'

In Belgium, where he qualified on the fifth row (Boullion the seventh) rumours now suggested he was being offered the Number 2 Benetton drive for 1996; some German television channels implied that the deal had already been struck. Rumours beget rumours: Sauber were supposed to have been talking to a wide variety of drivers, including Johnny Herbert, in case Frentzen did go.

In the race 'I wasn't making much progress and I was praying for rain.' It did rain, but a lap after Frentzen had pitted for a fresh set of dry tyres. Then 'when the track began to dry a little bit I started thinking about changing to slicks but I took the gamble to stay on wets.' It paid because four laps from the end he overtook Blundell to finish fourth.

Overleaf *The start at Hockenheim but a crash with Eddie Irvine was looming and a crisis was deepening* (ICN U.K. Bureau).

Inset *Signing autographs at Hockenheim* (Andreas Stier).

He was on the same lap as the winner, Schumacher, although Spa being so long – 4.3 miles/6.9 kilometres – that's deceptive. (Boullion was eleventh and had been lapped.)

At Monza, Sauber confirmed that Frentzen would be remaining with them for the 1996 season. Frentzen explained that the decision was 'not an easy one because I had interesting alternatives, which I gave serious consideration to in the course of the last couple of weeks. What tipped the scales was the fact that I want to reap the rewards of the hard work done all year long with Sauber and Ford.' He qualified on the fifth row (Boullion the seventh) – 'that was the best I could do so I'm happy' – and in the race finished third (Boullion sixth). It is true that Schumacher and Hill crashed out; true that Alesi retired with a wheel bearing problem after looking certain to win, all of which was to Frentzen's advantage. But he was on the podium.

'In the end I was looking at my dashboard and saying *there are still 15 laps to go!* I was calculating everything: going down with the revs [using fewer revs] the engine should be all right. In those moments, approaching your first podium finish, you are thinking quite a lot. I saw Mika in front of me and thought *if I push like hell maybe the engine will blow up or I could spin*, so I backed off.' Result: Herbert (Benetton) one hour 18 minutes 27.916 seconds, Hakkinen (McLaren) at 17.779 seconds, Frentzen at 24.321 seconds.

In Portugal he qualified on the third row (Boullion the seventh). 'It was a really good lap but maybe I got the benefit of a gust of wind. The top speed was 3kph up on the straight. The reason you can only do one flying lap here is tyre related so you have to be on it immediately. You can't put our sudden increase in performance down to one thing. We've made aerodynamic and mechanical improvements. It is detail work, not big changes. I admit I am surprised but it was very close: another couple of tenths slower and I'd have been seventh or eighth on the grid, which is more the level I was expecting. We found a couple of tenths at a test at Mugello recently, but I think I got the lap pretty right and it's very satisfying to split the Ferraris' – Berger's one minute 21.970 seconds (Frentzen one minute 22.226 seconds, Herbert one minute 22.322 seconds) and Alesi's one minute 22.391 seconds.

Let him tell the story of the race himself and both its starts. 'At the

Right *The start at Monaco, Frentzen in the middle of it all* (ICN U.K. Bureau).

France, where he finished tenth (Ford).

Into the Stadium at Hockenheim but the engine let go after 32 laps (Ford).

Peter Sauber and Frentzen at Spa, where he finished fourth (Ford).

first, someone hit me from behind and I spun off. Luckily I was able to get back to the grid where we found the car wasn't too badly damaged. We changed some parts but unfortunately my best set of tyres had gone. At the re-start I stalled the engine and had to get away last. I took a lot of risks to overtake people as quickly as possible' – eight on the first lap – 'and I used my tyres a little bit too much in the process.' He finished sixth (Boullion twelfth) and tempered his pleasure at gaining a point by disappointment he couldn't make better use of his highest grid position so far.

Interestingly Peter Sauber felt this was Frentzen's best race and explained why. At such a circuit, where overtaking is so difficult except at the end of the long straight, to rise from last to sixth 'without being helped by any retirements' was a genuine achievement. 'Sixth may not seem as brilliant as third at Monza but I rate it even higher because we proved that we have been able to get close to the top runners.'

At the European, run at the Nurburgring, he qualified on the fourth row (Boullion the seventh), set third fastest time in the wet on Saturday morning and explained that in such conditions the car felt fine. He was hampered by traffic on his flying laps in both qualifying sessions and would have been higher but for that. In the race he was given a stop-go penalty for jumping the start and, in drizzle, decided to stay on wet tyres. After 17 laps he tried to get inside Pedro Diniz (Forti) to lap him and the cars collided (Boullion spun off).

A quiet run-in to a big finish: at Aida for the Pacific Grand Prix he qualified on the fourth row (Boullion the eighth). 'I couldn't have gone any quicker.' In the race he finished seventh, a lap behind the winner, Schumacher. 'I have to say that the traffic at this circuit was really awful.' At Suzuka for the Japanese Grand Prix he was partnered by Wendlinger again. Boullion was being 'rested.' Frentzen qualified on the fourth row (Wendlinger the eighth). 'I should have been able to go much quicker but I had understeer in the last session.' He also suffered broken engines in the untimed morning sessions on each day. In the race he finished eighth, a lap behind the winner, Schumacher, despite a thump with Irvine at the hairpin (Wendlinger was tenth).

It left Australia in Adelaide where he qualified on the third row

Overleaf *Monza and he's on the podium at last, being sprayed with champagne by Herbert – who won* (Ford).

(Wendlinger the ninth) and in the race retired after 39 laps with a gearbox problem. But he'd driven a storming race until then, running second behind Hill for five laps.

'The bad news,' Welti says, 'was the fact of losing Mercedes at the end of 1994. That was terrible for the team. And the further bad news was that the Ford engine, which was supposed to be a good engine, was an absolute disaster in 1995. An absolute disaster. Obviously the team were learning Formula 1 and the team were young in Formula 1, just as Frentzen was, so he could accept the fact that 1995 was tough. The fact that the car was reliable helped.'

In December, Sauber tested at Jerez and Paul Ricard and announced that Herbert would partner Frentzen for 1996. Neither Wendlinger nor Boullion had survived comparison with him.

'1995 was a tremendous year – he was so strong he was keeping up the Sauber team's morale'

'I didn't have any problems with Heinz-Harald as a guy,' Herbert says. 'No worries. He's fairly quiet in some ways. We never had any relationship outside the sport and, to be honest, with a lot of drivers you don't have that. I'm not being critical of anyone, I am just pointing out that it doesn't always happen. Although we live directly opposite each other in Monaco – separate apartment blocks but they face each other and we are on the same equivalent floors – we never shouted over in the morning or anything like that. As a guy he's fine, easy to work with and the only thing I noticed was that when I was outqualifying him he started to get a bit agitated. Most of the time in his career up until then he had been quicker than his team-mates. It's always disappointing when you are outqualified by your team-mate, there's no hiding place from that.

'Sometimes maybe it affected him other ways too. Look at the situation at Williams now [July 1997]. Jacques Villeneuve is very much a mind player. I can be if I need to be, I actually find the mind games quite fun. In times when things are going well you try and play on your partner's weaknesses – with Heinz-Harald that weakness was basically me outqualifying him. The more I did that the more destructive it became. However it didn't affect the basis of our working relationship, no-no-no! The basis of the relationship is work, not friendship. It is a competition. At the end of the day with Jacques at Williams it's the same thing. Within the team, Jacques is slightly stronger that way [the mind games]. I think it shows because, as yet, Heinz-Harald hasn't got his finger on the pulse at all.'

Reflecting, Welti judges that 1995 'was actually a tremendous year for Frentzen, tremendous. He was really strong then, unbelievably quick with a bad car and a very bad engine. He was so strong that he was keeping up the team's morale. He was pushing, pushing, pushing on the technical side – absolutely the right thing to do – and it was a dream. There was a beautiful relationship between the engineers and himself, the management and himself. He was an adorable person in 1995! He not only helped the team a lot, he kept his sense of humour although during his hard years he learned that you have to be serious as well, you have to learn about the technical side, you have to speak to your engineer and the more you speak the more you understand.'

During this year Frentzen met his girlfriend Tanja. In an interview with *MAX* magazine he explained they'd met 'in my circle of acquaintances in Moenchengladbach. We went out with some friends.'

Did you make the first move?

'This was rather difficult. In the beginning it was very harmless. We went out to dinner, we talked to each other but nothing happened. Suddenly things changed when we sat in a cinema and watched *Forrest Gump*. During this film I fell in love with her.'

How important is a woman's erotic flair?

'For me it only works as a whole: the way a woman moves, the way she talks, the way she looks. It was above all Tanja's eyes which captivated me.'

The magazine tried to press Frentzen on 'Corinna Betsch, who is Mrs Schumacher today' and asked 'has Schumacher really pinched Corinna?' Frentzen replied: 'I will not talk about this, it's an old story.'

Now, moving into 1996, he faced professional life with chirpy Johnny Herbert, himself known as a fast man. As so often happens with new team-mates they were almost complete strangers. 'I must have

Overleaf – Life at the Summit '97

Main picture *Hungary, where bad luck robbed him.*

Inset *Frentzen and Williams technical director Patrick Head* (both ICN U.K. Bureau).

driven against him in sports cars,' Herbert says, 'but I didn't know him at all, no, not really.'

Frentzen also faced another season with Sauber needing vindication for his decision to remain. In the most direct way he needed Sauber to provide him with a car capable of podium finishes or the decision had been a mistake, had been another season lost to Father Time. The knowledge of this brings a tension to a driver and his team: they may start racing against themselves within the races to make the car competitive.

The new car (Sauber C15) was tested at Paul Ricard in mid-January, Frentzen covering 97 laps in three days and only one change of engine necessary when a problem appeared. He radiated optimism. They always do, all of them.

This is the story of one man's third season in the right place for some of the right and some of the wrong reasons with, for context, what Herbert was doing in the most direct comparison.

It opened at a new circuit, Melbourne, and Williams's newcomer Jacques Villeneuve from IndyCars took pole, Frentzen on the fifth row (Herbert the seventh). 'It was difficult to get the best out of my second set of tyres. I had gone out with them early in the session but I returned to the pits after the flag had been shown' – a Minardi was being removed after a spin. 'As a result my tyres had picked up too much dirt to be of good use later on.' He finished eighth, which was a lap behind the winner, Hill.

The South American couplet were unhappy. In Brazil he qualified on the fifth row (Herbert the sixth) and retired after 36 laps when an engine problem halted him. It was a pity because he'd been running sixth and a place on the podium seemed possible. In Argentina he qualified on the sixth row (Herbert the ninth). Although qualifying was windy he explained he was reluctant to put on extra downforce because 'we didn't want to sacrifice speed. It made the car very difficult to drive.' He spun repeatedly and in the race spun off after 32 laps when he'd been seventh.

At the Nurburgring for the European Grand Prix he qualified on the fifth row (Herbert the sixth) but spun after 59 laps when he'd been as high as fifth. 'My start was quite good and I immediately made places because the two Benettons didn't get away properly. I was able to overtake Martin Brundle after two laps and I was running for a long time in seventh place. It was no problem to stay at the same pace as the group in front of me. After my first pit stop I set my fastest lap of the race but in the middle of that stint I suddenly found I was unable to maintain my pace and rhythm. It became worse and worse and my second pit stop unfortunately didn't solve the problem. I have no idea what it was.'

At Imola for the San Marino Grand Prix he qualified on the fifth row (Herbert the eighth). 'It's a fantastic weekend,' he said, which one assumes was an attempt at irony. 'Since I arrived at the Nurburgring I've had a problem with understeer and there was quite a lot of it today [the Saturday]. Sure, we've improved but so has everyone else.' He was as high as seventh when a brakes problem halted him after 32 laps.

Monaco guards a tedious reputation for being a logical race – get pole, get the first corner right, win – when, because it is run through an illogical place for a Grand Prix, it is volatile and, cumulatively, the events of 19 May 1996 proved that beyond any doubt.

Frentzen qualified on the fifth row (Herbert the seventh) and said: 'There's no change. Overall I was quite content with the balance of the

Shadowlands, Portugal 1995 (Ford).

127

car. I gave everything I could but I couldn't improve on the time I managed with my first set of tyres. Starting from ninth position on the grid, it's going to be very close going into the first corner. It's a matter of getting through that without running into trouble and then seeing what I can do.' Evidently the car still suffered from pronounced understeeer, not to mention that lack of power from the Ford V10.

Twenty one cars set off into the embrace of a wet Monaco and all were to be squeezed, five on this opening lap. They crashed, *leaving 16 running*. Frentzen crossed the line fifth. The embrace tightened: after two laps Katayama (Tyrrell) hit a barrier, a lap later Ricardo Rosset (Footwork) had an accident and after five laps Pedro Diniz (Ligier) was gone with a transmission problem, *13 running*.

Frentzen tried to attack Irvine, immediately ahead, while simultaneously monitoring Coulthard, immediately behind and trying to attack him: a usual Monaco story involving inevitably the dynamics of bunching.

Berger's Benetton was gone after nine laps with a gearbox problem, *12 running* and lifting Frentzen to fourth place. The bunching endured for another seven laps, Frentzen cajoling Irvine, Coulthard cajoling

Sauber was serious.

Frentzen, then the dynamics moved into the volatility. At Ste Devote, Frentzen tried to overtake Irvine by going to the outside. In doing that he bumped the Ferrari's rear and was forced to pit for a new nosecone. 'It is always easy to be wise after the event but when I tried to overtake Eddie it was the right thing to do. He closed the door and I damaged my front wing. That was disappointing because I could have won.'

The pit stop made him eleventh, only Luca Badoer (Forti) behind. He ran eleventh for seven laps and then pitted for fuel and tyres – risking dry tyres. On lap 28 he set fastest lap at one minute 31.689 seconds, some ten seconds faster than the others on wets. After 30 laps Brundle (Jordan) spun off, *11 running* and lifting Frentzen to tenth. Olivier Panis (Ligier) collided with Irvine at the Loews hairpin and Irvine limped towards the pits, hoisting everyone up a place, Frentzen to ninth.

After 40 laps Hill's engine let go as the Williams was coming out of the tunnel and he shrieked into the escape road beside the chicane never to return, *ten running*, Frentzen to eighth. He stayed there for another 20 laps – to lap 60 of the 75 – when Alesi was gone with a suspension problem. That lap, too, Badoer and Villeneuve collided at Loews and although Villeneuve continued Badoer did not, *eight running*, Frentzen to seventh. Villeneuve struggled forward for half a dozen more laps until the collision damage finally claimed him, *seven running*, Frentzen to sixth.

Two laps later Irvine, still last, lost control and spun just before the approach to the tunnel; Salo in the Tyrrell helplessly rammed him and equally helplessly Hakkinen in the McLaren rammed Salo, *four running*, Frentzen the fourth of them, of course.

Five laps remained and Frentzen completed all but the last of them. Then, as one report put it succinctly: 'Safe in the knowledge that there was nobody in pursuit, the German coolly opted to pull into the pits rather than cross the line.' Panis, Coulthard and Herbert completed the 75 laps, Frentzen only 74.

To forego that final lap – when he could not be caught and would have been classified fourth even if he'd broken down – made me think initially that it was a clever tactical ploy. Then I wondered. I asked Welti what he thought.

'It was stupid, it was crazy. There were a lot of things happening in that race. He could have won that race no problem, because he was so

129

much in front of Panis and so much quicker than Panis. It would have been absolutely no problem to win it – but he would have been forced to wait behind Irvine. He couldn't overtake Irvine: first because it's Monaco, second because Irvine was in a much better car – no, a much faster car, I should say, not necessarily better. Frentzen should have waited for the first pit stops when he could have out-raced Irvine during them, come out ahead, got away.'

And coming in a lap before the end?

'That has everything to do with everything that happened in 1996. Frentzen decided to stay with Sauber because he believed in the capability of building a better car – and the car was better than the '95 car, although still light years from the Williams. We believed in the Ford V10 engine a lot and it was another catastrophe, not only because there was a big lack of horsepower – in particular at the beginning of the season – but also because of the driveability. So it was impossible with that car/engine combination and that somehow broke Frentzen. I am absolutely sure that that broke him: he realised the car wasn't good enough for his first win, he'd been absolutely sure his first win was coming and we all know how important that is.'

I asked Herbert: *was it a brilliant tactical move by Frentzen at Monaco?*

'It was more that he was a lap down anyway, so it didn't matter. I would still have finished the race because that's what I believe you should do, not just pulling off. He was almost unclassified but finished fourth, which is wrong. If he'd broken down on the last lap he'd have been fourth all the same.'

Peter Sauber conjured a lovely phrase to cover his team's exploits. 'Johnny drove an excellent and intelligent race and we're all delighted for him on his third place. Heinz-Harald produced some interesting television . . .'

If Monaco was bizarre, Spain almost equalled it. Frentzen qualified on the sixth row (Herbert the fifth) and had a genuinely spectacular crash in the Sunday morning warm-up, hammering into the tyre barrier by the pit wall and scattering the tyres. The race was run in a storm and Schumacher dominated it majestically – Frentzen fourth but a lap down, and one of only six finishers.

It can be quickly told after that: in Canada he outqualified Herbert but retired, 19 laps, a gearbox problem; in France he outqualified Herbert but spun off, a throttle problem; in Britain he outqualified

Monaco 1996 where he finished fourth, not least because only four finished (Ford).

Stinking wet Barcelona and he was fourth again (Ford).

Press Conference, Monza (Ford).

Herbert and finished eighth; in Germany he outqualified Herbert and finished eighth again. Hill won at Hockenheim and increased his lead over Villeneuve to 21 points but, despite that, rumours were circulating that Frentzen would replace Hill for 1997. Frank Williams said (pointedly, perhaps): 'Villeneuve is the only confirmed driver for 1997. Negotiations regarding the team's other driver will commence in good time.'

In Hungary, Herbert outqualified him and in the race he retired after 50 laps, electronics; in Belgium they started on the same row and finished the race at the same moment, embroiled in extensive bumping-boring-crashing from the start. Between Spa and Monza, the Williams team announced they were dropping Hill for 1997.

Because Formula 1 is pathologically secretive, and because each major move in the drivers' market – hiring or firing – invariably involves a conjunction of potentially conflicting interests, disentangling what really happened (and why) remains elusive in a way that, say, a football transfer never is. Does a French team insist on having at least one French driver? What if this French team is sponsored by a French oil company and wants a driver sponsored by a British oil company? And so on.

We do know that Frank Williams rated Frentzen highly enough to have tried to sign him in 1994; we assume that Damon Hill, poised to become World Champion, was re-negotiating with the (presumed) clout of a soon-to-be Champion; we can set this against the shadow of Schumacher. In 1994 and 1995 Hill had been outdriven by him, something which could – likely would – happen again the instant Ferrari produced a competitive car. Ah, but hadn't Frentzen taken Schumacher on in German Formula 3, hadn't he been faster than Schumacher in the Mercedes Junior Team?

At Spa, Frank Williams made encouraging noises to Frentzen.

In Italy Herbert outqualified him and he retired after seven laps, accident; in Portugal they started on the same row and he finished

Overleaf *A glimpse of what he was making the Sauber do* (Gunter Passage).

Insert *The most poignant picture. Harald Frentzen pays his respects to where Roland Ratzenberger crashed at Imola in 1994* (Gunter Passage).

seventh; in Japan he outqualified Herbert and finished sixth – only the third time in the season that he'd taken points. It gave him a total of seven, worth twelfth in the Championship (Herbert, four, fourteenth).

'I think in 1996 Heinz-Harald was completely changed and it was one of his bad years,' Welti says. 'It can be explained very easily. He was hungry like hell for his first win, he desperately wanted to win his first race – which is fair enough, and which made him quick, by the way. And he desperately wanted to win with Sauber because, don't forget, in earlier times Frank Williams and other team owners were realising his ability.'

A win would justify Frentzen's decision to remain for the three years and also justify everything that Sauber had been doing; but no driver could be blamed for seizing a drive with Williams and couldn't have been blamed any year since 1992, when the era of Williams superiority began. Certainly Frentzen had shown commendable (and in Formula 1 terms extreme) loyalty to Sauber.

The central point facing Frentzen at Williams was that if you have the best car you are expected to deliver a harvest of points, a lot of wins and probably the Championship, no excuses. But, before we reach that,

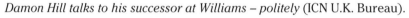

Damon Hill talks to his successor at Williams – politely (ICN U.K. Bureau).

here is a reflection by Herbert about speed – because nobody has ever doubted Frentzen has it in abundance and would need it at Williams.

What is this speed?

'A lot is confidence. The main driver you must examine in a question like this is Michael Schumacher, and his arrival in Formula 1 from, I suppose, obscurity: he was a sort of nobody in sports cars. However he got a very good car at Jordan and he did a good job at his first Grand Prix, then he went straight to Benetton and, even then, Benetton wasn't bad. He was finishing fifth, sixth – always in the points – which, in a way, you expect a driver to do in a car like that but he had a good relationship with Benetton. It was something that went on and on, it got stronger and stronger, he had no accidents, he was the rising star.

'They treated him very well, so the confidence got bigger and bigger and bigger. Frentzen was in the Formula 3000 wilderness. Then he got into Sauber, which was great for him getting into Formula 1 but it wasn't a top team so he had to work at it. Everyone said he was getting a little frustrated at the end of 1996, and sometimes frustration takes a toll. When he got to Williams it was like breathing fresh air: fantastic car, Championship chance, everything.

'Apart from the confidence, you have to make the car work. That involves its set-up and you've got to feel comfortable with the car. It's not just sorting out a bit of understeer or a bit of oversteer. Normally, for instance, a twitchier car is always the quickest and a car that is very easy to drive is always slower.

'Frentzen is very, very quick, one of the quickest in Grand Prix racing. In my opinion he went from a team that was very much family-oriented – if things did go wrong there was an arm round his shoulder, *never mind, we'll be OK next time* – into an environment at Williams that is very different. You've got to be your own man there, you've got to go searching to get the information, you've got to go searching or pushing to get the right things for your car and for your particular "team" within the team. Heinz-Harald didn't face that at Sauber, he got the arm round him in a family team which tried to make everything fair. I am sure they do that at Williams – make it extremely fair – but I also think they try and make the drivers work harder to achieve their own things.'

It was never going to be easy.

• CHAPTER FIVE •

Surface
tension

ON 4 SEPTEMBER 1996 Williams announced that Frentzen was joining them, in a press release which was stunning for what it did not say and flinty in what it did. Covering the departure of Hill, then at the height of his Championship battle, Frank Williams was quoted as saying: 'Damon has contributed greatly to the team both as a test and race driver – he has done an excellent job for us. I think his record speaks for itself, as very few drivers have ever approached his record of 20 wins in 64 starts. He will be missed by everybody at our Grove factory and we all wish him the best of luck for the remainder of this year, as well as the future.'

Frentzen would explain that at the Belgian Grand Prix at the end of August 'Frank told me the chances of driving for him next year were greatly increased. And then everything happened fast. Although there were several drivers on the market I took the risk of waiting for Frank's response. I must thank Eddie Jordan, with whom I was talking. Eddie knew of my contacts with Williams and he gave me time, which helped me enormously. My objective will be to win, certainly. If Williams have engaged me it's in the hope that I'll beat Schumacher. If not, what would I be doing here?

'People often evoke the era when we drove together in the Mercedes Junior Team but our rivalry is older than that. I knew Michael Schumacher in karting. We competed against each other in Formula 3 in 1989 and Mercedes Juniors but since then we haven't had comparable equipment. For what it's worth, I say he is one of the best

Right *With Jacques Villeneuve preparing to confront 1997* (ICN U.K. Bureau).

drivers in the world, he has reached a very elevated level and to take on such a champion is an enormous challenge. As a youngster he was extremely aggressive on the track. Then he refined his style, although that doesn't stop him attacking like a demon. The most impressive thing about him is his ability to adapt his style to the car he is driving. We have seen how easily he has done this with the Ferrari. It's an exceptional quality.'

Frentzen first tested the Williams at Estoril in mid-October and although he coped easily enough with a couple of hundred laps and one minor blip – he damaged the nosecone – he had to accommodate a change of style: left-foot braking. The whole thing was so different. 'I thought I was sitting in a Formula 1 car for the first time.'

He approached the opening race in Melbourne speaking of a 'very new step in life,' qualified next to Villeneuve on the front row (Villeneuve pole) and, once Villeneuve was out in an accident with Irvine, led and after the pit stops ran second to David Coulthard (McLaren) until, with three laps left, he plunged off. 'We knew this circuit was going to be hard on brakes, but I think we didn't realise how difficult it would be and in the end they went off. I didn't really feel the brake performance dropping.'

In fact, Frentzen's problems seemed to begin at the next race, Brazil, because he couldn't be held accountable for the brakes in Australia: round Interlagos Villeneuve took pole but Frentzen only qualified eighth. 'I'm pretty disappointed. It's a matter of not getting used to the qualifying trim and the car. On the other hand I feel reasonably competitive in normal conditions, more so than in qualifying. Of course it is going to be difficult to start from this grid position.' And was. He made a poor start to the race, which was stopped after a crash, and made another poor start at the re-start. 'I was behind the Jordans and couldn't find a way to pass. About halfway through I had gear shift problems.'

Williams technical director Patrick Head was quoted as saying: 'Heinz-Harald is very disappointed. He's had a pretty miserable weekend and the easy thing would be to pour scorn on him but we need to find out what the problem is and solve it. There's no doubt he has the talent but we are not using it at the moment.'

Villeneuve won Brazil.

In Argentina Frentzen put the car on the front row (Villeneuve pole). 'I went to England after Brazil,' Frentzen would say, 'to work on my set-up with Patrick Head and my race engineer Tim Preston and consequently ended up with a better one for qualifying.' In the race he ran second behind Villeneuve until lap 5 when clutch problems halted him. People were already speaking of a continuing nightmare.

Villeneuve won Argentina.

John MacDonald was quoted at length in Chapter Three about the good old days when he ran Alan Jones because that very same combative, self-confident, self-sufficient, self-assertive Jones drove for Williams from 1978 to 1981, winning 11 races and a World Championship. Many years later someone asked Frank Williams if, before the races, he advised Damon Hill on tactics. Williams said no he didn't and in this regard the team had been 'spoilt' by Jones, who didn't need any telling and just got on with it. This reply implies that

Was the Frentzen era opening?

ROTHMANS WILLIAMS RENAULT TEAM 1997

Williams feels a leading Formula 1 driver should not require anybody to advise him on tactics. It could make life difficult for a driver from a 'family' environment.

Nor could time itself be disregarded. In 1978, when Jones came, the trio – he, Frank Williams and Patrick Head – were all the same generation and all getting there for the first time. In the 19 years since, Williams had had World Champions in Rosberg (1982), Piquet (1987), Mansell (1992), Prost (1993) and Hill (1996). The team had designed, produced and raced some of the best cars ever to go round a racetrack. By definition, it could be nothing but daunting for a new driver coming in, especially a driver who had only finished as high as third in a Grand Prix, and that only once.

Frentzen now gave a Jones-like response to his predicament. At Imola he qualified on the front row (Villeneuve pole again) and said: 'At the moment things are going more in my direction. I've made progress since Argentina and I am getting much more out of the car. I wish I had had another lap because on my fast one I was slowed by a Prost' – the former French champion was now running his own team.

In the race he took the lead during the first pit stops and only lost it for a lap during the second stops. Schumacher was behind him but he took that pressure. In short, he suddenly looked like a front runner, exercising control rather than travelling round the rim of the possible. 'A great feeling to win. I am speechless. This is a hard track on brakes and I was concerned about them after my experience in Melbourne. I didn't really push towards the end but I tried to maintain a certain speed because I could see Michael coming up behind. Also I was concerned it might start to rain.'

He described setting a quick lap at Monaco as 'a delicate balance of finesse and brute strength.' In free practice 'I made a mistake and hit the wall.' Then he took the first pole of his Formula 1 career. Schumacher had held it provisionally but, said Frentzen, 'I was trying to get a bit more grip at the front and we went for quite a risky set-up.' For the race – wet but, a weather forecast insisted, drying soon – both Villeneuve and Frentzen had their cars prepared for the dry. It was a team mistake, and an understandable one. 'We started the race believing that the rain would slow down after about half an hour. It didn't. I made a pit stop to change tyres hoping to find some more grip

Good luck (ATP).

Driving for Williams was always going to be intense (ICN U.K. Bureau).

but I couldn't. I drove over the curb of the chicane and slid into the guard rail.'

The nightmare continued. In Spain he was eighth. 'I was very disappointed to be honest because I couldn't push at all. I had very good tyre wear all weekend but during the race, for some reason, my rear tyres blistered quickly. This meant that I had to come into the pits three times.' In Canada he finished fourth. 'I had a difficult start. I had early problems with my left rear tyre so I had to reduce my speed a lot and pit for another set of tyres. The second set was perfect, no problems. I felt I could push until the end and that I could have done the race on one set of tyres. That is disappointing to know.'

In France, Frentzen was second behind Schumacher. 'I was astonished by Michael's speed at the beginning. It made me think he was going for a three-stop strategy. I pushed very hard. When the rain started it was a critical point to make a decision on my tyres. I kept changing my mind, so the mechanics were going in and out of the garage. Finally I decided to stay on slicks and because it stopped raining that proved to be the right decision.'

At Silverstone, mid-season, it was time to take stock. Approaching the British Grand Prix Schumacher led the Championship with 47 points from Villeneuve (33), Frentzen third on 19.

I mentioned to Jochen Mass, these days a television commentator, the theory that Williams hired him as the man to take on Schumacher which, arguably, Hill had failed to do. 'Frentzen was not and is not frightened of Schumacher. Schumacher also understands the qualities of Frentzen's driving. Don't forget that, as the years go by, guys develop in different ways, and Schumacher has developed the fastest way. He knows what he can do and what he cannot. Frentzen is perhaps a little less secure – for the time being. Williams is not an easy team and even Senna found it difficult to be there.

'When I look at Frentzen now I am concerned that he is not going better but, then again, Villeneuve is also not doing too well. I think the Williams team has lost a bit of an edge and they have to find it again. The mistakes haven't all been driver mistakes, so it's not easy to say. Heinz-Harald has surprised me quite pleasantly because I thought he would falter – or I feared he would – at the beginning of the year. He was under a lot of pressure and a lot of expectations. Apart from the first race, which he lost because of a failure of the brakes, I thought

The controlled frenzy of the pit stop for tyres and fuel, just the way it was with Sauber (all ICN U.K. Bureau).

A little friendship, a little glamour in Canada (both ICN U.K. Bureau).

that with all the pressure he would get too nervous and react to it in a negative way but he came through very strong and that's good. If he believes in himself and doesn't give up, if the team gets its wits together . . .'

Frentzen himself outlined part of the difficulty he – and Williams – confronted. 'Michael is not in a situation to be comfortable yet because there are a lot of races to go and we are right up there. Ferrari has had a good strategy from the beginning of the season: to score a lot of points consistently even when they are not winning races. They have had no technical problems and only accidents have caused them not to finish. I think their strategy now will be to do the same thing. They don't have to win every race, just score points. In our situation we have to make up a lot of points in each race.'

What about you and the car?

'Basically I have reached a level where I can handle the "circumstances" around the team to get more out of the car or get the

147

maximum out of its technical ingredients. I am coming closer to the limit percentage-wise in the use of the car.'

A driver can be forgiven for thinking that getting into a top team solves all his problems, whereas he encounters a new set of problems.

The unique start to the French Grand Prix where Schumacher, Frentzen and Schumacher's brother Ralf filled the first three places of the grid (ICN U.K. Bureau).

'You always have targets if you want to reach something, and the next target is always different to the target before. I am trying hard now to win races, people expect that and it is a pressure I did not have before. I always give a lot of pressure to myself to get the maximum out of the car and out of the circumstances. I also tried very hard when I was with Sauber, tried to get into the points . . .'

But at Sauber you had everything to gain. A good result was really good.

Here people say you should get good results.

'You reach a level where only 100% success counts and this is the level now. Only that 100% counts.'

Are you comfortable with that?

'Well, that's the way it is. That's always the way when you reach the top. A sprinter who goes for a world 100 metres record – everything below the world record is a disappointment, so every time you have to run quicker and quicker. And eventually you reach a level where you have reached a limit and you can't go beyond it. So with the Williams team, for example, you have a team which used to win races and, now, not winning races isn't a happy situation. If other teams are building themselves up, we have to get used to it.'

'He must learn everything at once, while dealing with the criticisms and politics in a calm manner'

Are you surprised you and Jacques haven't had more 1–2 finishes?

'It's not only that the others are building up but we have had some problems: the accident of Jacques and my brakes at Melbourne, clutch problem in Argentina, gearbox problem for Jacques in Imola. There was always a situation where one car was not going to finish.'

Frank Williams spoke publicly and was in unusually diplomatic-enigmatic mood, albeit including some substance at the end.

If you want one of your drivers to win the Championship you may have to tell the other one to slow down – for example Frentzen took points off Villeneuve in the last race.

'I think I will be very happy to find myself in that situation. I'll worry about it then.'

Is that in the foreseeable future?

'I wish I could see into the future.'

Bernard Dudot [technical director of Renault Sport] has suggested that Rothmans Williams Renault would be leading the World Championship if Damon was still driving for you. What do you feel about that? Do you agree?

'Well, that's a new comment to me. I do realise that by the time of Silverstone there are comments flying around morning, noon and night. I'd need to think about the answer before I put my foot in it.'

How long do you need?

'I have to get back to work very soon . . .'

Would there be a possibility of a return for Damon?

'In 1998 it is probable we will not be making any driver changes. That is to say that, today, I will not announce who my driver line-up is going to be. You'll have to wait for that, but to repeat myself: it is probable we will not change drivers and it is therefore probable that Damon will not be in the team next year.'

However, Frentzen's plight was hardly improved by the weekend although he qualified on the front row (Villeneuve pole). He stalled on the grid, forcing a re-start – and forcing him to join it from the pit lane. As that opening lap unfolded he overtook a couple of cars and then collided with Verstappen. Race over. This seemed to be moving towards genuine crisis with, if it continued like this, Frentzen's position in the team completely untenable.

Before Hockenheim, Frentzen said slightly enigmatically: 'After Silverstone I know how it feels to make a mistake at Williams. I knew this time would come and I'm glad it is out of the way so I can get on with putting the record straight and scoring some good World Championship points.' In fact, genuine crisis came ever nearer. He qualified on the third row (Villeneuve the fifth). This was, as someone pointed out, the worst Williams qualifying performance for two years, since Spa in 1995. Frentzen barely had anything worthy of the word race. In the first corner he and Irvine collided. Their versions of what happened collided also.

Irvine said he was in the midst of the best start of his Grand Prix career, already up from tenth on the grid and contesting fifth place. 'I felt a knock on my left rear wheel, which punctured the tyre and damaged the rear bodywork beyond repair.'

Frentzen said he was 'on the outside and Irvine came on the inside. We drove around the corner together but when I accelerated out I had no place to go and the only way to have avoided an accident was to go over the grass. I couldn't go on the dirt at that stage to leave Eddie alone on the track, so we collided.'

At this point in the season Dudot poured sympathetic words on Frentzen's plight. 'It is not easy for a driver to come into a team like Williams. There is a huge technical and cultural gap between a team

Overleaf *You treasure the moments of peace* (ATP).

like Williams and Sauber. Whether it is on the chassis or the engine side, Frentzen is being asked things he has never been asked before. He must learn everything at once, while dealing with the criticisms and all the politics in a calm manner. He is beginning to learn and take everything on board. I don't see why he should be compared to Schumacher. Drivers are human and react differently to different situations.'

In Hungary he qualified on the third row (Villeneuve the front) and now straightforward ill luck struck at him. A third of the way through the race he had the lead and, given the nature of the Hungaroring where overtaking is rare, victory beckoned. Instead a fuel tank connector flew off the Williams, making refuelling impossible and retirement inevitable.

The background to this retirement was significant. Frentzen had selected a harder compound tyre than Villeneuve, a 'decision which was questioned a lot,' he would say in an interview with the German newspaper *Bild am Sonntag*. However, his stature within the team grew when they saw it was the right decision. He revealed that 'it is not simple to go your own way within Williams because they believe everything they say is correct. But I have my own ideas of how to set the car up and that led to quite some misunderstandings. Most of all Patrick Head wants to teach me things all the time. At the start I was rather quiet about it and then I went to Frank Williams and said that it cannot go on like this.' He insisted he would be staying with Williams for 1998.

At Spa, a race which began very wet and dried, it was a question of when you changed tyres. 'Because of the rain at the start we went with wet tyres,' Frentzen said, 'and that was OK at the beginning but the cars with intermediates were quicker. That cost us places.' He pitted on lap 8 for slicks and 'started gaining places immediately until I was stuck behind Berger for a while but then I managed to overtake him. I came up to the next group and I was behind Coulthard and Herbert. I managed to overtake them, too. I came close to Hakkinen but never near enough to have any chance of overtaking him.' Frentzen was fourth, but from a mature, controlled and when necessary decisive drive.

Right *Harnessing the power of the Williams and its Renault engine* (ICN U.K. Bureau).

As the season moved towards its climax – Villeneuve taking on Schumacher for the Championship – Frentzen seemed to be amplifying the impression he'd created at Spa. During the three successive races afterwards – at Monza, in Austria and at the Nurburgring – he drove like a settled man who didn't have to strain to prove anything anymore.

It was true that after these three races he was holding third position in the World Championship, albeit only a point in front of Alesi and five in front of Coulthard – but it remained third place, and there are worse places to be.

In sequence he finished third after a solid drive in the Italian Grand Prix, repeated that at the new A1-Ring circuit and was also third in the Luxembourg Grand Prix.

A torrid, frantic start by many of the runners there surging and compressing into the first corner after the start: amidst it he and Villeneuve brushed wheels and he was pressed back to fourteenth. 'When we touched I knocked off the ignition button with my ankle. I was very disappointed at that moment.' He settled, he took his time, he kept the car smooth and he began a fight back 'although it was difficult to overtake. I got past Gerhard Berger into third place because we planned our pit stop perfectly.'

The next day Williams confirmed he'd be staying for 1998 and it was now clear that, after a career whose direction and shape had often been almost bizarre, he could be a genuine challenger for the World Championship.

• APPENDIX •

Heinz-Harald Frentzen's career statistics

P = pole;
FL = fastest lap;
DIS = disqualified;
DNF = did not finish;
DNQ = did not qualify;
Can = cancelled;
WDN = withdrawn by team

The karting years

1981
German Junior Championship   1

1984
German Karting Championship   2

1985
South African GP   2

The car years

1986
Formula Ford 2000

1987
Formula Ford 2000 (Reynard)

Hockenheim	4
Zolder	FL/1
Nurburgring	P/2
Zandvoort	P/3
Mainz	P/1
Brno	P/3
Avus	DNF
Zeltweg	5
Salzburg	FL/2

*Championship: R. Kelleners 470 pts
(430 counting), Frentzen 338,
M. Bartels 307*

European FF2000 (Reynard 87SF)

26 July	Hockenheim	3
27 Sept	Zolder	FL/6

*Championship: J.J. Lehto 128,
P. Warwick 82, J. Alcorn 70,
(Frentzen joint eighth, 18)*

1988
Opel Lotus German Challenge except
GM/Lotus Euroseries – Eu)

3 Apr	Zolder	P/FL/DNF
24 Apr	Hockenheim	P/4
8 May	Nurburgring	P/1
29 May	Avus	P/1
5 June	Mainz	P/2
17 July	Nurburgring	P/1
24 July	Hockenheim (Eu)	DNF
14 Aug	Zandvoort	P/8
27 Aug	Spa	1
4 Sept	Nurburgring (Eu)	P/2
11 Sept	Zolder	P/1
25 Sept	Estoril (Eu)	P/1
2 Oct	Jerez (Eu)	1
16 Oct	Hockenheim	DIS

Opel Lotus Championship: Frentzen 128 pts,
A. Kalff 112, J. von Gartzen 101
Euroseries: M. Hakkinen 126,
H. Larsen 125, A. McNish 77
(Frentzen sixth, 56)

1989

German Formula 3 (Reynard-VW except
Hockenheim, Nurburgring in April and
Diepholz – Dallara VW; Macau, Reynard-
Spiess)

16 Apr	Hockenheim	11
30 Apr	Nurburgring	6
28 May	Avus	5
11 June	Brno	9
18 June	Zeltweg	2
2 July	Hockenheim	1
9 July	Wunstorf	1
29 July	Hockenheim	P/FL/2
6 Aug	Diepholz	P/1
3 Sept	Nurburgring	7
24 Sept	Nurburgring	DNF
30 Sept	Hockenheim	P/2
26 Nov	Macau	DNF

Championship: K. Wendlinger 164 pts,
Frentzen and M. Schumacher 163

1990

Formula 3000 (Reynard-Mugen except
Donington, World Sports Car
Championship, Mercedes C11)

22 Apr	Donington	16
19 May	Silverstone	21
4 June	Pau	21
17 June	Jerez	17
24 June	Monza	17
22 July	Enna	5
28 July	Hockenheim	6
19 Aug	Brands Hatch	7
27 Aug	Birmingham	19
2 Sept	Donington WSCC	2
23 Sept	Le Mans	DNF
7 Oct	Nogaro	DNQ

Championship: E. Comas 51 pts,
E. van de Poele 30, E. Irvine 27
(Frentzen joint sixteenth, 3)

1991

Formula 3000 (Lola-Mugen)

14 Apr	Vallelunga	DNF
20 May	Pau	DNF
9 June	Jerez	12
23 June	Mugello	6
7 July	Enna	5
27 July	Hockenheim	DNQ
18 Aug	Brands Hatch	12
24 Aug	Spa	5
22 Sept	Le Mans	DNF
6 Oct	Nogaro	DNF

Championship: C. Fittipaldi 47 pts,
A. Zanardi 42, E. Naspetti 37
(Frentzen fourteenth, 5)

1992

Le Mans (Lola-Judd); Donington and
Suzuka 30 Aug, FIA Sportscar World
Championship (Lola-Judd); All-Japan
3000, Suzuka 27 Sept (Lola-DFV); Fuji,
Suzuka (Lola-Mugen); All-Japan Sports-
Prototype Championship, Fuji 4 Oct and
Mine 1 Nov (Nissan-R91CK)

20/1 June	Le Mans	13
19 July	Donington	4
30 Aug	Suzuka	R
27 Sept	Suzuka	6
4 Oct	Fuji	R
10 Oct	Fuji	7
1 Nov	Mine	3
15 Nov	Suzuka	3

1993

Japanese F3000 (Lola-Mugen)

21 Mar	Suzuka	R
11 Apr	Fuji	R
9 May	Mine	R
23 May	Suzuka	8
1 Aug	Sugo	14
15 Aug	Fuji	Can (fog!)
5 Sept	Fuji	P/2
26 Sept	Suzuka	FL/10
17 Oct	Fuji	FL/12
14 Nov	Suzuka	5

Championship: K Hoshino 32 pts,
Irvine 33 (32 counting) R. Cheever 31
(Frentzen ninth, 8)

1994

Formula 1 (Sauber C13 Mercedes-Benz V10)

27 Mar	Brazil, Interlagos	R
17 Apr	Pacific, Aida	5
1 May	San Marino, Imola	7
15 May	Monaco, Monte Carlo	WDN
29 May	Spain, Barcelona	R
12 June	Canada, Montreal	R
3 July	France, Magny-Cours	4
10 July	Britain, Silverstone	7
31 July	Germany, Hockenheim	R
14 Aug	Hungary, Budapest	R
28 Aug	Belgium, Spa	R
11 Sept	Italy, Monza	R
25 Sept	Portugal, Estoril	R
16 Oct	Europe, Jerez	6
6 Nov	Japan, Suzuka	6
13 Nov	Australia, Adelaide	7

Championship: Schumacher 92, Hill 91,
Berger 41 (Frentzen thirteenth, 7)

1995

Formula 1 (Sauber C14-Ford Zetec-R V8)

26 Mar	Brazil, Interlagos	R
9 Apr	Argentina, Buenos Aires	5
30 Apr	San Marino, Imola	6
14 May	Spain, Barcelona	8
28 May	Monaco, Monte Carlo	6
11 June	Canada, Montreal	R
2 July	France, Magny-Cours	10
16 July	Britain, Silverstone	6
30 July	Germany, Hockenheim	R
13 Aug	Hungary, Budapest	5
27 Aug	Belgium, Spa	4
10 Sept	Italy, Monza	3
24 Sept	Portugal, Estoril	6
1 Oct	Europe, Nurburgring	R
22 Oct	Pacific, Aida	7
29 Oct	Japan, Suzuka	8
12 Nov	Australia, Adelaide	R

Championship: Schumacher 102, Hill 69,
Coulthard 49 (Frentzen ninth, 15)

1996

Formula 1 (Sauber C-15 Ford Zetec-R V10)

10 Mar	Australia, Melbourne	8
31 Mar	Brazil, Interlagos	R
7 Apr	Argentina, Buenos Aires	R
28 Apr	Europe, Nurburgring	R
5 May	San Marino, Imola	R
19 May	Monaco, Monte Carlo	4
2 June	Spain, Barcelona	4
16 June	Canada, Montreal	R
30 June	France, Magny-Cours	R
14 July	Britain, Silverstone	8
28 July	Germany, Hockenheim	8
11 Aug	Hungary, Budapest	R
25 Aug	Belgium, Spa	R
8 Sept	Italy, Monza	R
22 Sept	Portugal, Estoril	7
13 Oct	Japan, Suzuka	6

Championship: Hill 97, Villeneuve 78,
Schumacher 59 (Frentzen twelfth, 7)

1997

Formula 1 (Williams FW19-Renault V10)

9 Mar	Australia, Melbourne	FL/R
30 Mar	Brazil, Interlagos	9
13 Apr	Argentina, Buenos Aires	R
27 Apr	San Marino, Imola	FL/1
11 May	Monaco, Monte Carlo	P/R
25 May	Spain, Barcelona	8
15 June	Canada, Montreal	4
29 June	France, Magny-Cours	2
13 July	Britain, Silverstone	R
27 July	Germany, Hockenheim	R
10 Aug	Hungary, Budapest	FL/R
24 Aug	Belgium, Spa	4
7 Sept	Italy, Monza	3
21 Sept	Austria, A1-Ring	3
28 Sept	Luxembourg, Nurburgring	FL/3
12 Oct	Japan, Suzuka	2
26 Oct	Europe, Jerez	6

Championship: Villeneuve 81,
Schumacher 78, Frentzen 42

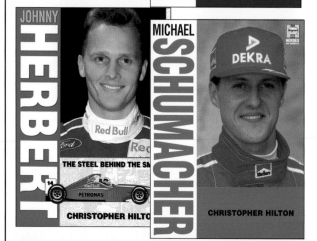
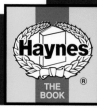